GOD'S PRICELESS
TREASURE

DEBORAH STARCZEWSKI, D.TH.

CHP Creation House Press

Dear Anita,
Steve, Elizabeth, Samuel,
God is still
in the miracle
business!
I thank God for you all!
Deborah
10/3/12

GOD'S PRICELESS TREASURE by Deborah Starczewski

Published by Creation House Press (CHP)
Charisma Media/Charisma House Book Group
600 Rinehart Road
Lake Mary, Florida 32746
www.creationhousepress.com

The views expressed in this book are the author's and do not necessarily reflect the position of the publisher.

Select CHP products are available at special quantity discounts for bulk purchase, for sales promotions, premiums, fund-raising, and educational needs. For details, write CHP, 600 Rinehart Road, Lake Mary, Florida 32746, or telephone (407) 333-0600.

Names and composites of individuals mentioned in this book have been changed to protect their identities. Any similarities between persons mentioned in the book and persons known to the reader are coincidental and are not intentional.

Unless otherwise noted, all Scripture quotations are from *The Subject Bible*, Complete Topical Study and Reference Edition, King James Version, Copyright 2006, by Power Publishing, Corp., McDonald, TN 37353

Scripture quotations marked NKJV are taken from *The Revival Study Bible,* New King James Version, Copyright 2010, by Armour Publishing, PTE., Ltd., Singapore.

Scripture quotations marked NLT are taken from *The New Living Translation Study Bible,* Copyright 2008, by Tyndale House Publishers, Inc., Carol Stream, Illinois.

Scripture quotations marked NASB are taken from the *New American Standard Bible,* Copyright 1960, 1962, 1963, 1968, 1971, 1972, 1973, 1975, 1977, 1995, by the Lockman Foundation.

Scripture quotations marked NIV are taken from *The Holy Bible,* New International Version, Copyright 1973, 1978, 1984, 2011, by Biblica, Inc.

Scripture quotations marked CJV are taken from *The Complete Jewish Bible,* Translation by David H. Stern, Copyright 1998, Jewish New Testament Publications, Inc., Clarksville, Maryland.

Scripture quotations marked WYC are taken from the Wycliffe Bible, 2001 by Terence P. Noble.

Scriptures quotations marked AMP are taken from *The Amplified Bible,* Copyright February 1, 2001, by Zondervan.

Cover Design by Nathan Morgan
Interior Design by Terry Clifton

Visit the author's website at www.starministriesinc.com.

Library of Congress Control Number: 2011934193
International Standard Book Number: 978-1-61638-664-1
E-book ISBN: 978-1-61638-665-8

12 13 14 15 16 — 9 8 7 6 5 4 3

Printed in the United States of America

CONTENTS

FOREWORD   by Neal Speight, MD...v

FOREWORD   by Dr. Rick Ross vii

ACKNOWLEDGMENTS ix

INTRODUCTION xi

CHAPTER 1   God's Development Plan 1

CHAPTER 2   Communications and Conflict 5

CHAPTER 3   Hunger and Thirst.................................. 9

CHAPTER 4   Abandoned and Discarded.......................... 13

CHAPTER 5   Our Search for Love............................... 19

CHAPTER 6   Emotional and Verbal Abuse....................... 23

CHAPTER 7   Sexual Sin and Seductions Exposed.................. 31

CHAPTER 8   Seasons in Life.................................... 39

CHAPTER 9   The Path of Restlessness........................... 43

CHAPTER 10   Lovesickness...................................... 47

CHAPTER 11   Stumbling in the Dark 53

CHAPTER 12   Obedience and Blessing 55

CHAPTER 13   Knowing God as Father 67

CHAPTER 14   The Secret to Fulfillment.......................... 75

CHAPTER 15   Priceless Treasure 81

CHAPTER 16   A Broken Heart................................... 85

CHAPTER 17   Holy Boldness after the Desert...................... 89

CHAPTER 18   Secret to Success 93

CHAPTER 19   When Life Does Not Turn Out as Planned 99

CHAPTER 20   God Knows Your Name........................... 105

CHAPTER 21   God Knows and Understands Your Fears 107

CHAPTER 22   Seeing God's Provision 109

CHAPTER 23   God Cares Deeply about the Details 115

CHAPTER 24   Total Trust 117

CHAPTER 25   Wisdom for Wives 119

CHAPTER 26   Wisdom for Husbands 123

CHAPTER 27   God's Timing. 125

CHAPTER 28   We Are a Team with God 127

CHAPTER 29   Prayer and Worship 133

CHAPTER 30   Feeling Forsaken. 141

CHAPTER 31   Marriage 145

CHAPTER 32   Spiritual Application 151

CHAPTER 33   Satan's Attack on Your Faith. 157

CHAPTER 34   Emotional Distress. 161

CHAPTER 35   Children with Broken Hearts. 173

CHAPTER 36   Tactics of the Enemy 179

CHAPTER 37   The Tapestry of Life 183

CHAPTER 38   God Raises Us Up from the Ashes. 191

CHAPTER 39   Ministry of Healing. 195

CHAPTER 40   Total Trust and Confidence 201

CHAPTER 41   God Achieved the Victory 205

CHAPTER 42   Disappointment 213

CHAPTER 43   Choice 217

CHAPTER 44   God Is Not Caught Off Guard. 221

CHAPTER 45   God Created You to Be an Eagle 223

CHAPTER 46   Doing Things with God. 229

CHAPTER 47   Nurture Your Relationship with the Lord. 231

CHAPTER 48   Vital Steps. 235

CHAPTER 49   God's Extravagant Love 239

CHAPTER 50   Step Out in Faith 245

CLOSING COMMENTS 249

BIBLIOGRAPHY 251

ENDNOTES 253

ABOUT THE AUTHOR 257

FOREWORD

When I met Deborah nearly ten years ago, little did I know just how profound her influence would be in my life. With the exception of my mom, no woman has moved the direction of my life toward the Lord more significantly than this dear friend.

As a result of obedience in the midst of her desert experiences, I believe God has filled Deborah with wisdom that we would all do well to take to heart. Do you ever ask yourself why you seem to end up in the same situation over and over again? Why you fear the future, or are frustrated with relationships? Could it be that God whispered in your ear and touched your heart, yet you were not willing to be obedient to His nudge? As a result did you see your hopes, finances, or relationships destroyed?

I have had the privilege of watching one of God's greatest servants lead by example. Being obedient to God's call, she has displayed the fruit of a truly spirit-filled life. He sent her to my office for medical care. At least, that's what I thought. I came to realize that as with so many others, God sent Deborah to minister to *me*. As the years unfolded, time and time again I saw her speak into my life and into the lives of others either wisdom from the Word or a direct revelation from His heart to ours. When we listened we were blessed, and when we did not, God made it clear the consequences of disobedience.

Without a doubt, knowing Deborah has been one of the most supernatural experiences of my life. From the interpretation of dreams, to the decision to marry, from direction in my career, to long-distance travel, the Lord has used her to confirm what I already knew and at times turn me around when I refused to follow Him. I thank God for her obedience and presence through these years, for had she not listened to the Lord, she would have never called to warn of upcoming events in my life, or interpret dreams that unfolded just as she said. Through the practice of her faith, she has allowed me to see that God does indeed care intimately about what happens in all of our lives. What a delightful journey it has been.

In this book you will find the wisdom of one tried by fire—one who has earned the right to speak because of her obedience and devotion to the God of creation. I encourage you to read every word and let them warm your heart as they have mine.

To my dearest friend I say thank you for your service and for imparting these precious words of wisdom to us all. I can never repay you for what you have done in my life through your service to Him.

—NEAL SPEIGHT, MD
The Center for Wellness
Matthews, NC

FOREWORD

For the last seven years we have been blessed to watch Deborah live out the principles in *God's Priceless Treasure*. This book will bring supernatural courage to everyone who is facing a challenge. The battle sometimes seems overwhelming, but the Mighty Warrior has gone before you. The choices we make affect the outcome of each battle. These inspiring stories and principles will build your faith, and the scriptures will challenge you to be bold and courageous! Deborah has deep insights into the heart of God, and you will not only enjoy this book but also greatly benefit from reading it.

—Dr. Rick Ross
Lead Pastor
Concord First Assembly, Concord, NC

ACKNOWLEDGMENTS

"For you are a holy people to the LORD your God, and the LORD has chosen you to be a people for Himself, *a special treasure above all the peoples who are on the face of the earth.*"
—DEUTERONOMY 14:2, NKJV, EMPHASIS ADDED

Almost every parent would agree that his or her child is the most precious thing in the world, and that is the way God views you. I was blessed to have wonderful, godly parents! My father went home to be with the Lord on January 30, 2010, and I thank God for my precious mother who still encourages me. I dedicate this book to my precious parents and my beloved husband in honor of all their love, encouragement, direction, and faith in me to finish what God has called me to do. I thank God that He gave me wonderful parents who showed great love to my sister and me and extended family.

I thank my husband for his loving support and faithfulness through the writing and finishing of this book. God has such amazing timing that He showed me the release would be August 21, 2011, my father's birthday. God has perfect timing. I thank God for my mother's continued faith and loving support of our family. She is a priceless treasure and a picture of humility. I thank God for my entire family and for the wonderful friends He has placed in my life. Thank you to Kelli and Atalie for the endless hours of reading and faithfulness to help me finish.

I pray that the words on the pages of this book that God has given me will fan the flame in your heart for God. May He restore you and give you double for all your trouble. May He show Himself strong on your behalf and bless you beyond your greatest dreams!

His love and mine,
Deborah Starczewski

INTRODUCTION

Feeling alone is like being in your own private wilderness, in the desert, or in your Garden of Gethsemane. It is a place of surrender to God's will in your life. This feeling can lead to despair and defeat and discouragement. Sometimes we feel alone during specific seasons of our lives: when we deal with marital issues, the stress of being single after the death of a spouse, the stress of a career change or loss of a job, the empty nest syndrome when our children leave home, health issues, and when our body begins to slow down and we are unable to do all the same things we used to do. Sometimes the simple stress and pace of life make us feel overwhelmed and alone. You may be elderly and feel all alone. You may also feel all alone after years of invested time in an organization and be at a turning point in your life, feeling like no one notices you anymore, with the new team in place. Whatever the case, God still has a plan for your life!

The enemy's plan is to isolate us and make us think that no one cares. He also wants us to think no one has ever walked in our shoes. If this is how you feel today, you do not walk alone in your struggle. Not only are you surrounded by men and women who feel the same way, you are also surrounded by men and women of God who will come alongside you to walk with you through this valley and help hold you up. The Bible tells us that "two are better than one" and that we can help hold each other up. (See Ecclesiastes 4:9–12.)

Just as Jesus was led by the Holy Spirit into the wilderness, have you ever thought that, just perhaps, you too were led to your own wilderness by the Holy Spirit? This is where we become stronger and discover a deeper intimacy with God. Alone times are actually not obstacles but are seasons of growth if we embrace them rather than running from them and complaining about them. It is when we draw closer to the heart of God through these difficult seasons that God shows us a new way of trusting Him that we have not yet experienced. It is in these seasons of life that we have a fresh encounter that gives us a glimpse of the amazing love and compassion of the living God.

Now come with me as we learn to climb out of the pit of despair and treasure every single moment of our alone time with God in the desert. We will learn to grow rather than stay in grief. We will also learn to love again rather than blocking God and others out as well.

We will learn to worship at the well in our desert, our own alone time. We will learn to embrace the journey of spiritual growth, even in the midst of the greatest pain we think we have ever felt—when our husband or wife has been stripped away by the enemy or another tragic loss. Our seasons of struggle will soon be seen as an opportunity for expedient spiritual growth. This is where we learn humility and childlike faith, which are keys to the kingdom of God.

When you learn to love alone time, the seasons of restlessness will soon fade away, and you will be empowered to pursue the dreams that God placed in your heart a long time ago. Hidden dreams will resurface, and you will have renewed strength as you learn to wait upon the Lord, trusting Him to deliver you. (See Proverbs 20:22.)

After you are on the other side of your desert or wilderness, you, too, will be equipped to help lift others up who are walking through the places you have walked in life's journey. This is where you find confidence in God and learn to trust Him! I pray God will use this book as an instrument of change to give you passion for your purpose, and open your eyes to a greater revelation of His amazing love. I pray God rekindles the flame in your life to an even greater sense of destiny than you have ever experienced before.

CHAPTER 1

GOD'S DEVELOPMENT PLAN

He Is at Work on All of Us

W hen you pan for gold or mine for treasure, you dig in the dirt. We are God's priceless treasure. We all have hidden treasures in us as well. God uses our storms in the desert and our wilderness experiences to develop our character. This is where we learn to trust and truly know Him.

I started out naming this book *The Harlot at the Base of Duel Mountain* with a subtitle *Are You a Proverbs 5 or Proverbs 31 Woman?* The Lord spoke to my heart to change it because there are men walking through severely painful times as well. No one wakes up one morning and decides to destroy his or her life. No one plans to wind up in a desert of brokenness or destruction.

Have you ever walked through a time when you felt as though your heart had been ripped out of your chest, shattered into a million pieces, and thrown out in the yard to be run over by the next passerby? Have you felt like your whole world was crumbling around you in the midst of great despair in your life? Welcome to Duel Mountain Road!

A duel is a prearranged combat between two persons, fought with deadly weapons according to an accepted code of procedure, or any contest between two persons or parties. There is a battle going on all around us, whether we choose to face it or not. There is a battle for our physical, emotional, spiritual, financial, and relational life. Satan attacks your mind. The enemy does not fight fair. He does, however, use legal access when we give it to him. When we willfully walk in rebellion against God's ways, we open the door to the enemy.

The enemy comes to steal, kill, and destroy. He is subtle and knows your weaknesses. He will use lust to draw you away from God's plan for your life. Proverbs 5, 6, and 7 give us strong warnings to avoid the path of destruction. God has a great plan for our lives, but we must choose. (See John 10:10.)

We recently walked through a period of two years before the truth was revealed about our daddy's health. We would sit on the front porch and watch the beautiful fields and meadows that God created for our enjoyment. We loved to watch the horses behind the fences grazing on the grass. God had given our family a beautiful home and a peaceful place to admire God's beautiful creation. We had family gatherings, cookouts, and many wonderful memories to last a lifetime. Dad began talking to me about going home. I am talking about his eternal home, not moving.

We lost our father on January 30, 2010, to lung cancer and Guillain-Barré syndrome as we surrounded his bed for seventeen days without leaving his side. God gave us the most wonderful experience of sharing his final days with him, surrounding him with love and adoration. God positioned family, friends, particular nurses, and doctors in place to help us through this time as well.

In the midst of this valley, we also walked through another desert place with someone very dear to us all. Remember those horses I mentioned that we liked to watch? Here goes! The grass looks greener on the other side— just ask Moose, Leo, and Bandit. If only they could talk! Do you know anyone who thought the grass was greener on the other side of the fence or street? We have all heard the reason the grass is greener on the other side; it is due to more fertilizer. How many people do you know who have thought that with a new marriage partner, a new job, a new home that turned out to be a money pit, or a career change that moved you away from friends and family, it would be better than what they have currently?

I guess you are wondering why I said, "Just ask Moose, Leo, and Bandit." These are the names of three horses that grazed in the fields and gazed at the people all around. If only they could talk, wow, we would be shocked. However, the precious Holy Spirit reveals all hidden truth and shows us things to come! He is our comforter, informer, teacher, and the list goes on.

When someone commits a serious sin, which affects many families, it leaves the people involved in a desert place to pick up the pieces. Have you ever found yourself there? Whether it was you or someone dear and close to you, we have all been there.

I was telling my sister to just wait and see how fast God would answer our prayer about a financial situation with our ministry office landlord. He had waived one-half month's rent, but when my husband talked to the landlord's wife, apparently she was unaware. When my husband in turn phoned me, I told him I was not going to say anything because they were so gracious to work with us, to start with, for our ministry during the recent change in the economy that had affected everyone in some manner.

I prayed and asked God to speak to him to remind him. Not ten minutes later, our landlord phoned me to tell me his wife came to speak to him about the rent because she sensed something wasn't right when she spoke to my husband. She asked him about the month's rent in question. He told her that he had told me to waive the half-month's rent for the following month. I just about cried because of the goodness of the Lord, but more importantly to me was how fast this man responded to God's prompting.

I explained to my precious sister that God was at work on her prayer request about a negative situation she was facing, but because people are blinded by the enemy and sin it would take longer. When people are living in sin, they don't hear God very well or see clearly. Sometimes they know the right thing to do, but they ignore the warnings and walk right into a desert due to wrong choices.

Within seconds God gave us a personal sign that confirmed and revealed that He heard my sister's prayer and was at work on the situation. Wow! God is amazing. God's natural manifestation showed us by making us aware of His presence and His work on her behalf: simple but revealing! This gave my sister the hope and faith to continue believing God. I assured my sister He is at work on all of us.

No sooner than we have a victory, the enemy tries to distract through circumstances. One year from the passing of our father, my sister's son had his horse stolen in the early hours of the morning. My nephew was devastated at the timing and could not believe this tragedy. He cried for two days. My sister and nephew learned through this circumstance that Satan tries to set us up to be upset and broken due to others' sin.

Sin opens the door for the enemy and can cause people to operate in manipulation. Satan blinds people to lead them down a wrong path. We would do well to remember that the Bible says:

> For our struggle is not against flesh and blood, but against the rulers, against the authorities, against the powers of this dark world and against the spiritual forces of evil in the heavenly realms.
> —EPHESIANS 6:12, NIV

When the enemy divides a marriage and family, great pain begins. However, God can work a miracle in the midst of any situation. It takes three to make a marriage work: God and both the husband and wife at the same time!

Lack of communication opens the door for sin, and we end up in the desert with sand in our eyes. Sand represents the opinions of others rather than trusting God and His Word. We have blind spots that open the door to destruction where we find ourselves in the desert of desperation all alone, or so it seems. Conflict then lack of communication is the order for chaos. Wrong thoughts start in the mind. When we choose to act on wrong thoughts, they become seeds, and we end up in a harvest of bad consequences. Remember, whatever is birthed in sin will not last. It produces death. When people run from God and choose to go their own way, they are in open rebellion against God. Lack of communication swings wide the door of destruction. However, with a proper foundation in God, all things are possible!

CHAPTER 2

COMMUNICATION AND CONFLICT

Order in God

Proper communication is like the oil in your car that keeps it running smoothly. Without oil, the car begins to knock and make noises that let you know you have a problem. Would you ignore the warning light in your car that indicates your engine needs checking? I can assure you if you do, it will eventually "blow" the engine!

Neither should we ignore the warning signs of improper communication that lead to conflict. We all know there is no marriage or relationship without conflict. Most know from experience that conflict can produce stress if not properly dealt with. Any relationship or marriage without any conflict would be quite boring, to say the least, and not much fun at all. Without knowing how to communicate properly, there will be a deep lack of intimate conversation and sincerity in marriage. Such a marriage might as well be a roommate situation where people are just going through the motions, and therefore are reluctant or afraid to express their individual dreams, desires, personal feelings, goals, personality, or own spiritual giftedness.

A truly healthy and fulfilling marriage is going to be filled with open communication; while at times it is passionate, lively, and creative, at other times differences may occur along with conflict. The enemy tries to drive a wedge between husband and wife. He can use problems and people to achieve this goal of division. You will either be an instrument of good or an obstacle in any situation.

You can have healthy disagreements that arise naturally because both individuals maintain their own unique perspectives, ideas, and opinions. We must remember that we are all different! When spouses don't communicate, they tend to find someone else who will listen and talk with them. This opens the door for emotional bonding with the opposite sex that can lead to destruction. You should never develop an emotional relationship with anyone of the opposite sex when married. You must set proper boundaries to guard your relationships. Talk to your spouse and put him or her first so your marriage will last.

In order to have proper relationships, people need to communicate and recognize everyone has a different personality. Debates arise as every individual has his or her own preferences and reasons (whether real or perceived) for holding onto them. Much conflict could also be avoided, not only in marriage, but also in family and business settings, if people would learn to communicate properly.

Discussions, disagreements, and debates do not need to degenerate into an emotional war that perpetuates an ongoing atmosphere of dispute and anxiety in the home. People either blow up in rage or give the cold, silent treatment in relationships where there is no honor. Disputes in the home can create a home filled with chaos and disorder. This produces an atmosphere of stress for the entire family.

Neither does there need to be distancing and isolation just because people disagree. Discussions should reach a conclusion without heated arguments. Disagreements should resolve into agreement when we learn to master communication and submit to God. Debates should come to a decisive course of action in healthy relationships where there is proper order in God. We want to learn to work through conflict so that we can actually get better, not just feel better. Conflict produces growth and change. Change keeps us alive and at work on our relationships. Marriage takes work but is so worth the effort! We must learn to honor and value one another, even if we disagree.

We must choose to learn better communication skills. The best teacher is Jesus. When you learn to master communication, you will be equipped to manage conflict in a godly manner, whether in your marriage, relationships, or business. The Bible tells us: "A soft answer turns away wrath, But a harsh word stirs up anger. The tongue of the wise uses knowledge rightly, But the mouth of fools pours forth foolishness" (Proverbs 15:1–2, NKJV).

When we do not have God as our focus, we do really stupid things. We learn to operate in fear, doubt, destruction, and lies rather than faith and belief in God's great plan for our lives. When healthy couples understand the power of the *covenant of marriage* from God, there is a safe harbor and sense of trust that enables them to be totally honest with each other. Without this, there is lack of love and intimacy.

Choose to remain calm and gentle when confronting conflict, and your lifestyle of communication will not only become contagious, but also you will win more battles against the enemy with kind words and proper tones. Remember, the enemy comes to steal, kill, and destroy. If something is bothering you, learn to talk about it without accusation.

Choose to speak wisely and make sure your words are accurate and actually truthful. Learning to remember that God is the ultimate judge, our conversation will be laced with love and forgiveness, even when confronting wrongs. Use your words to promote healing instead of agreeing with the adversary. Stay teachable yourself and be open to correction. Learn to apologize quickly and make wrongs right. Two wrongs do not make a right. Deposit value into others by the words you choose to speak. Show respect for others.

Wrong words promote dishonor and insecurity. Women need security and men need respect. Women need affection and men need sex. When a man is prideful and arrogant and does not include his wife in the finances, this creates an atmosphere where true God-given intimacy is not possible. It actually instills fear into the wife concerning her future.

All married couples, therefore, face the challenge of learning to disagree agreeably, which provides a safe harbor and an atmosphere for positive, genuine unity, instead of strained relationships that lead to silence, avoidance, and destruction, which is ultimately the plan of the enemy. Once that path is taken, it doesn't take long to arrive in the desert.

When either the husband or wife does not know they are safe and able to share their heart, they are headed for a desert. When children are not allowed to express their feelings, they are headed for trouble. We also have communication conflicts with our family, friends, and coworkers. We must learn that words are powerful and learn to choose our words carefully. Words have the power to build or destroy. When we realize the power of our words and ask God for a hunger and thirst for righteousness, we then have the ability to live successful lives.

CHAPTER 3

HUNGER AND THIRST

Only God Can Fill the Void

The enemy uses the same tactics as he did with the Israelites to bring destruction. They grew tired of their leader and made a golden calf to worship. They experienced hunger and thirst in the desert. People fall for the same traps today. Materialism, entertainment, and social distractions are all a part of Satan's schemes to trap or lure the youth of this generation away from family and God's best. The same is true with adults. What is big enough to fill the hunger and thirst that lies deep in the souls of this generation? What can we do to help our children and grandchildren see God's way and win their hearts? How do we present the gospel to the next generation? How can we show God's love to our spouse, our children, those in our family, and our neighbors? How can we show God's love when people we love do really stupid things and make bad choices?

People make bad choices when they do things their own way and ignore God's Word and His warnings. The void that was created in each person's heart was placed there by God, and only God can fill it. The amazing love of God far surpasses all human reasoning and understanding. The sense of excitement that the God of the universe loves us is the only satisfaction that will sustain, overwhelm, and amaze us to the point of propelling us to do greater things for God, in the way of career, and to point others to Jesus.

God is the only one who can sustain that kind of hunger and thirst in each of us.

The same hunger exists in adults as well as youth. This vital need to know God is the same need in all people. Everyone needs to know this loving God who has created all things for His glory. We all need to be introduced to His majesty as He is the only one capable of filling the gap that is evident in all. He is a loving God who wants to be everything to us as we trust Him to the fullest.

When we are searching to fill the void or gap on our own, we can waste our lives pursuing other things, parties, seeking to please others to winning the approval of others, sports, entertainment, affairs, and anything else that temporarily fills the void. This creates a sense of loss, aloneness, and an unquenchable thirst that is not easily satisfied. This pursuit can lead to despair until we have a glimpse of the amazing love of God.

In marriage, when God is not the focus, one or both spouses can seek everything but God, ending up in the desert of divorce.

When we are searching to fill the void through success, we can get a wrong attitude and forget God, resulting in disastrous consequences in business. Perhaps you have climbed the ladder to success and find yourself at the top of a building with a beautiful window office, and now the business has closed! You may have lost your entire retirement fund and feel overwhelmed. Many of you reading now might find yourselves there. Perhaps you feel like you don't know what God is doing in your life and feel at a loss. You are just the one God is speaking to...so listen with your heart!

Everyone has the same need to know this awesome God who loves us so much He sent His only Son Jesus Christ to redeem us from sin. People of all ages need to know the deep abiding love of Christ. He is the only one who can provide the glimpse of hope that sustains and fills the void through a relationship with Jesus Christ. The hunger and thirst that have been placed in every person are placed there by God, and therefore, can only be filled by God.

Several years back on one of our trips to Israel, I remember stopping to take some time to spend with the Lord in the Garden of Gethsemane where Jesus wept. The sacredness of the time there was amazing as well as the experience of knowing I was kneeling where Jesus knelt. The next morning I sensed in my spirit I needed to call Judy, a dear friend of mine, who lived in Charlotte. I phoned her to learn that God had given her a dream at the same time in Charlotte that I was in the Garden of Gethsemane. She said she was awakened from her sleep hearing my voice saying, *"Judy, Judy, this is a heartfelt cry from Jerusalem"* and then she woke up. What an amazing God. I knew Judy was going through some difficult times in her life, and God let her know He saw her place of despair. That is the love of God, my friend. He made it evident to her and confirmed her dream or vision through placing her on my heart to call.

One step of obedience can change a person's life. When people feel alone, a phone call or a note can demonstrate the love of God. He goes out of His way to make His love evident. God exhibited His love in response to Judy's hunger and thirst for the things of God while she was in her own personal desert. God goes to extreme measures to make His presence known to us on a personal basis!

CHAPTER 4

ABANDONED AND DISCARDED

God Still Calls

The Samaritan woman who had apparently been abandoned five times by her husbands and did not trust men anymore, found herself at the well all alone at mid-day, but Jesus met her there. During this time period and culture, men could have their wives stoned if there was infidelity. Therefore, this tells me she must have been barren and discarded. The religious people of the day probably made fun of her and spoke negatively about her as the scripture indicates she came when no one else would be at the well. I can only imagine the shame she must have felt! If she had been in a place of happiness and abundance, she would not have met Jesus.

We see in John 4:4 that Jesus needed to go through Samaria. This need to go through Samaria was not merely a geographical consideration, but a divine encounter for this woman with a broken heart. Because she was lonely and came to the well when others did not, she was met there by Jesus. He gave her "living water." (See John 4:5–26, NLT.) Jesus saw her heart and her value. He gave her life, and she shared her story with an entire town. She became an evangelist for God by sharing her story to everyone. Based on the world's standards, she was probably considered a least likely candidate, but God chose her Himself!

UNMARRIED AND PREGNANT

Hagar was unmarried, pregnant, and running from home when she lay down by a desert well and prepared to die. She thought no one understood her situation and that no one truly cared. Can you imagine being in her situation? Rather than meeting death that day, she met the God of the universe, who created everything, and He gave her strength to return home, give birth to her child, and live the rest of her days in God's promises. If Hagar had found her peace in another man or a friend to console her, she would have missed her divine encounter with God, "the God who sees" (Genesis 16:13, NLT).

Are you beginning to notice the same pattern emerging through these two women in the Bible? Are you starting to see? Perhaps, you too, find yourself in a place of desperation. Maybe you have lost your job, your home, or your retirement. Maybe you have been married and divorced and still carry shame. Maybe you have ended up in a financial desert through wrong associations. Whatever the case, God is still at work in your life. Cry out to God. Don't get caught in the trap of reasoning, doubt, and unbelief. The enemy will tempt you to complain, moan, and reason. Pay attention when the enemy tries to discourage you. It is always just before a breakthrough. Don't give up on God.

Both of these women in Scripture found themselves in a place of despair, their own private wilderness, tired and empty, and in a place of hopelessness. But God, in His amazing love and compassion, met them at the place of hopelessness and gave them hope, at the place of their brokenness or feeling of being empty, He gave them abundance. The woman at the well found herself sharing her story because she was so full from one encounter with this man named Jesus. She was just a woman sharing her story that revealed the heart of God to all the people in her town.

Have you had your own personal encounter with Jesus?

GOD STILL CALLS

...the angel of God called to Hagar from heaven, "Hagar, what's wrong? Do not be afraid!"

—GENESIS 21:17, NLT

Are you at a place in your life where you wake up feeling alone, tired, run down, in a place of depression from all of life's demands and circumstances, to wondering "what's the matter with me?" We all come to the place where we need rest from overload, burnout, worry, fear, anger, self-pity, striving, or just trying to do too much to please others. In the day and age in which we live, the high pace that is demanded, and the constant contact with everyone can make for a stressful day. The enemy uses distractions to pound away at us so we have no quiet time to hear Him. No matter how many calls come in or how many people are around, we can all experience extreme times of aloneness when we have been wounded or abandoned by someone who vowed to love us for the rest of our lives.

You may be weary from plotting revenge because you were deeply wounded in your soul by a spouse that cheated. The Bible says, "Do not say, 'I will recompense evil'; Wait for the LORD, and He will save you" (Proverbs 20:22, NKJV). You may be someone who manipulates people and circumstances to get your own way. You may be worn out from striving to excel at your work to get credit or attention. In all of these places, we can lose our self-worth and begin to feel shame and a sense of despair.

Rather than allowing other people to affect your self-image, worth, and confidence, learn to hold your head up because of who you are in Christ. You have no reason to hold your head down in shame. There will always be someone who wants to ridicule, judge your heart, make fun of you, and prevent you from moving forward through your desert or wilderness, but pick yourself up and trust God to help you through.

The devil may use your coworkers, trusted friends, business associates, school teachers, and unfortunately, sometimes other Christians to try to drag you down, but you don't have to agree with the devil's plan to defeat you. Remember that Jesus was "despised and rejected of men" (Isaiah 53:3).

If you feel overlooked, disregarded, and thrown out like the trash, you are just the one God is looking for to use for His purposes in the earth. God spoke to my heart that all the people listed in Hebrews chapter 11 in the "Hall of Faith" also found themselves in the "Hall of Flame" through trials and alone times in the desert. Isn't that a great word from God? God had a great plan for every single one of those people. He has great plans to use you as a vessel of honor for His glory and demonstration of His mighty power too. He delights in taking our broken lives and carefully putting them back together brand new just to demonstrate His great love! Don't allow the devil or any people around you to make you think God has abandoned you. We are all a work in progress. None of us have arrived to the place of perfection.

HEALING AFTER DIVORCE

Sometimes we can also get wounded in the church due to religious spirits and people not operating in the love of God. When someone thinks they have arrived at a place of perfection with God just because they may not have gone through divorce or fallen into some other specific sin, they are operating in a religious spirit like the Pharisees and Sadducees.

There was a time when some churches looked down on people who had walked through divorce. There are some who say they don't believe in divorce. Divorce is not a question of believing or not believing. It can happen to anyone.

Jesus spoke of divorce in the Bible, so therefore we know it happened. It is not the unpardonable sin, and you don't have a Big D of shame and disgrace on your back. I don't think anyone wakes up one morning and decides that if and when they get married, they will get a divorce. We live in a fallen world that is full of sin. Divorce happens because of hardness of one or both hearts.

If you have lusted after someone while you are married, according to Jesus, you have already committed adultery in your heart. The church is supposed to be a healing station for the perishing, not a place to finish someone off. Thank God for wonderful churches, pastors, and ministers today. You are not alone.

You may currently feel all alone and abandoned, but God has not abandoned you. There are plenty of wonderful churches that love people, love God, and pass it on. We want to be the church that passes on the redemption, grace, and mercy of God through Jesus Christ! We need to share our stories to the lost and hurting so they will know they are not alone.

No matter what stage of life you find yourself in, you are truly not alone. God is with you, even in the darkest night of the soul. He is close to the brokenhearted. He is moved with compassion for you! He is walking with you through this valley or desert place you find yourself in right now.

He directs and orchestrates our days in such a manner that He lets us know He has changed the entire course of the day to make us aware of His Holy Presence. He is so amazing. He whispers His love to us! He is everything to us! When you feel like you are in a place of despair, you can choose at that point to stay planted where you are, grow and bloom, or you can run to and fro looking for something else to fill your days. It is in the wilderness or desert of the soul that we find our hope in Him. This is the place where we learn total dependence upon Him, the one and only true and living God. This is where we find the *Living Water, Jesus Himself.*

When you face a choice to either die in your desert or face life, embrace the pain, and grow, you will find that God is right there to comfort you during these alone times. He goes overboard to make His presence known. He sees everything and cares! God's greatest present is His presence.

God knows exactly how to let us know He sees our location. The God of the universe is the greatest GPS for life. **G**od's **P**ositioning **S**ystem is always the best. He will connect you with the right people in His perfect timing. The Bible tells us that Jesus is the "Great Shepherd," the "Perfect Leader," and the "Savior of the World"!

After you are on the other side of your desert or wilderness, you, too, will be equipped to help lift others up who are walking through the places you have walked in life's journey. Let's trust God, gain strength together, and embrace our times of refreshing and spiritual growth as we embark on this painful journey that leads to abundance in God. Begin to pray:

God is all I want. He is all I've ever needed. He is all I want. Lord, help me know You are near! Lord, draw me close to You and never let me go. I choose to lay my pain, my plans, my problems and my life down to You so that You may pick me up and show me Your plans and path of abundance for me as I embrace Your Word in my life.

Lord, help me to see Your hand and heart in every matter. Help me to hear the sound of Your voice at the slightest whisper at the door of my heart. Help me to become stronger in my alone time with You, the lover of my soul! Help me know You are near!

CHAPTER 5

OUR SEARCH FOR LOVE

"You will seek Me and find Me when you search for
Me with all your heart."
—JEREMIAH 29:13, NASB

S ome women have the luxury of staying at home with their children with
their husband carrying the financial responsibility, while others have
families with both parents working to provide for their family and maintain
the home. Women can become so alone while raising their children that
they totally forget their husband's needs as a man and husband. Other
times, stay-at-home moms can get to the place they think they have raised
the children, forgetting the luxury of a husband who is the provider. Either
extreme results in disaster if not dealt with properly.

The husband will think his wife cares more about the children than
him and thus puts the children above him. There are some men who put
their children above their spouse, resulting in a similar end result. Neither
way is proper in God's plan. God is supposed to be number one and then
the husband. The wife comes after the husband and then the children.
When we operate in mutual submission, deferring to the husband's final
say if we can't come to an agreement, we stay under God's protection plan
for the family. Children will grow up and have healthier lives themselves

when they see the proper love exhibited between their parents, providing mutual respect and order. Without respect there is no order. Where there is no order, there is chaos.

Usually, in a home with a wife who places the children above her husband, you will find no respect and a bossy wife who likes to get her way. When a husband is married to a wife like this, affairs can occur as he needs respect and does not find it in his own home. He can feel as if he has worked long hours to provide and comes home to a nagging wife. If children always get their own way, they can grow up to be spoiled, resulting in a disastrous marriage or career. There are many variables.

Children grow up and repeat what they see and hear. If parents speak negatively at the dinner table about others, they will do the same. Children learn and get their emotional needs met primarily from their parents. When parents have no boundaries and are still searching for something to fill the void in their lives, children grow up without learning proper boundaries as well.

We are all searching. Feeling lonely at times in a home can result in despair and propel you into a pit of depression. Women sometimes resort to gabbing conversations for endless hours on the phone, to soap operas, to reading romance novels that only lead to false hopes and lies. These are only forms of adult stimulation as a result of being in the home all day.

Men resort to going out with the guys, to Sunday afternoon football games, to chasing other women at bars and office meetings, pornography, to extended weekend trips with the guys that can lead to affairs. When a man has always traveled and then takes a job where he is home every evening, he has lost his cave time or his own alone time that all people need. This can result in bickering and constant nagging from the wife who does not understand his extreme change in career. By the time both realize there is a problem, they may find themselves in the middle of a desert.

Men love to be greeted the same way we are welcomed by our pets— wagging tails, close touches, and the anxious panting at the door to signal our mate we are glad he is home. Instead, women sometimes pounce on their husbands with a "to-do list" a mile long, and complaining about their day without thinking about how his day might have been. Men on the other hand, can come through the door leaving their shoes on the floor and collapse in their chair in front of the television with their own remote control.

This is why it is imperative to communicate, and I recommend going through a couple's workshop on a regular basis before and during marriage, like relationship checkups. Communication is like the oil in a marriage. Check your own oil level! How are you doing in the communication department?

It is also vitally important to schedule date nights and time away where we can reconnect and bond. It is imperative to lifelong relationships. All relationships take work.

We all have our path to walk alone, and it helps when we have clarification of what we are in search of along the way. When we become sure of who we are in Christ and strengthen ourselves in His Word, we find that people with all sorts of problems flock around us because of His strength in our weakness, our compassion for others, our smile, and His presence in our lives. When we find our strength in searching the Bible and develop our own spiritual disciplines, such as meditating on God's Word, fasting, and praying, we will find spiritual strength and confidence. This confidence comes because we have found Him in our search in our own personal desert and have learned to walk alone with Him.

It is in our quiet time with Him that we become strong and learn a life of obedience. Blessing is on the other side of obedience. We are all in search of the blessing. Our long walks through struggles are what strengthen us and make us totally aware of our dependence upon Him, our assurance in Him, and our confidence in knowing Him. Our alone times give us an opportunity for spiritual growth. The stronger we become spiritually, the less we react emotionally and the more we respond properly according to God's ways! We learn to actually trust God.

CHAPTER 6

EMOTIONAL AND VERBAL ABUSE

Choose to Be a Victor and Not a Victim

You may be reading this now and have suffered emotional abuse. Your spouse may be telling you that you are selfish, that you are a fool for your relationship with Jesus, or criticizing your every move. Living under constant scrutiny damages the soul and causes one to have broken places in the heart. When men speak down to women and get angry quickly, there is normally a reasonable amount of guilt somewhere. Angry people always blame their victims and say things like, "She made me angry" or "If he or she had not said that then I would not have said what I did." They are always pointing their finger and never actually taking responsibility for the loss of their temper.

When a person has a spirit of anger that has gone on for a long time, it becomes a stronghold and a place of danger, not only to him or her but also to everyone in the family. The kids grow up with stomach issues, and the wife usually has health problems that go undiagnosed for years. A husband can also have health issues and can get so tired of the anger that he just walks out. Due to the amount of stress that is placed on a spouse through the spirit of anger and rage, one can develop severe health problems and a feeling of despair. If you are married to a verbally abusive person, the damage is far greater than physical abuse in many cases. Physical abuse can take less time to heal than emotional abuse. The impact of verbal and emotional abuse may be far greater than cuts and bruises, and neither is of God.

God hates abuse, and he hates it when the husband covers his wife with violence. I know there are women who are verbally and emotionally abusive as well. In most cases, however, it is the husband abusing the wife or a man abusing the woman. When a man has committed adultery and has had affairs without repentance, this can leave the wife with an enormous amount of anger and hurt. In order for healing to occur, trust must be rebuilt, and repentance is necessary for restoration!

DOMINANT MALES

One root cause for dominance is overcompensation for something else missing in a man's life. When a boy grows up with an absentee father or no father in the home at all, he finds later in life that he lacks the appropriate knowledge and wisdom of how to properly love a woman. When a young boy grows up with a dominant or overbearing mother, or has negative experiences with women, he may lack confidence. Our environment plays a huge role in life. What people experience as a child can cause ignorance or insecurity in adult life and may be partially the reason for much overcompensation.

Anger and intimidation include attitudes, actions, body language, looks, or other expressions of anger or rage, which terrorize, intimidate, threaten, or control another person through fear.[1] Anger and intimidation also include attitudes, actions, body language, looks, or other expressions of anger or rage that are directed toward a person's loved ones, pets, or cherished personal possessions, which control another person through fear.[2] For example, a man who works but doesn't want to help pay the bills and spends his money on beer and dope for himself, yet gets angry and yells at his wife and kids when they need something, is also abusive. It is verbal and financial abuse.

Men who sometimes seem to be arrogant, angry, and obnoxious, and may be very controlling, are men who might feel insecure around women. When young boys experience rejection at a young age or have an absentee father, they sometimes grow up to be very controlling. Control is rooted in fear. These experiences have the tendency to produce men who are afraid of being controlled by women and feel like they must always be in control themselves. These men can actually have good hearts but need counseling. This is why I highly recommend counseling and marriage retreats. They are excellent ways to refresh your outlook in life and rekindle the flame of love in your marriage.

When a person does not know the reason he or she reacts to certain situations, it is difficult for healing to occur. We need to learn and understand how the things we have experienced from our childhood can cause problems in adulthood. In most cases, forgiveness needs to occur in the heart, and we must recognize we have a problem, admit the problem, and seek God and counsel to bring change. Many relationships have been destroyed due to silence and avoidance.

Let me share about a couple I mentored years ago...

I WANT MY WAY

Robert was a very attractive man who drew much attention when he entered any room. His wife was beautiful and loved life. Robert liked to be in control and did not want to include his wife in any decisions. He said things like, "This is my life and I'll do what I want to do without your advice or opinion" while having many affairs over their extended marriage. He was secretive and made her feel worthless. Each time she thought things were starting to get better he would do something that caused her great heartache again. They had six beautiful children who loved to be in church and excelled at everything, or so it seemed.

Robert had abused his wife Maggie with outbursts and name calling for their entire marriage. She got to the place where she could not sleep and always had this sense of dread about how he would treat her when she came home from work. He was heavily involved in Internet pornography for many years and seemed to have been delivered from that addiction when another major problem arose.

Robert decided to purchase a rather large dog without Maggie's input and secretly drove to another state with two of their children to pick up the dog while Maggie was at work. When she walked through the door and saw the dog, her heart sank into despair. Just when she thought he was starting to change, he proved by his actions he had to be in control and dominate the household. Maggie found herself in the desert of pain again.

A few months passed and then it happened. Maggie received the horrible phone call at work informing her that the dog had viciously attacked a neighbor's child and nearly killed the little girl. The little girl was taken by ambulance to the hospital and had extensive plastic surgery and counseling for the trauma. From the tragic event, to the lawyers and court case that followed, which affected the entire family, Maggie realized Robert had opened the door to the enemy by his secrecy and doing things without her input. He refused to talk to her about it and grew silent as the weeks went by. Robert always said, "I want my way." This time his way did not pan out like he had hoped.

As God opened the door for me to speak with this couple, I explained to Robert that Maggie was like the little girl lying on the sidewalk with her precious little hands about her face as the dog viciously attacked her, ripping the flesh from her little body. Maggie had lived like that for over twenty years, never knowing when Robert would viciously attack her with his words, have another affair, or walk through the door and be emotionally abusive.

Due to Robert's silence and unwillingness to include his precious wife in the decisions, he had opened the door to the enemy to steal, kill, and destroy. Thank God Robert woke up and realized that he was about to lose his family due to his unwillingness to surrender to God's perfect plan for marriage. Robert and Maggie went through mentoring, workshops, and extensive counseling. Robert realized he had always wanted a dog as a child, but his mother would never let him have one. He had a soul wound and was reliving his childhood in his marriage. He thought the dog would cover his pain. Pain is a symptom indicating something is wrong. It was this tragic event that forced Robert to deal with his issues. God healed Robert and Maggie and brought restoration to their family. Robert and Maggie are still together today and travel extensively sharing their stories as they minister together. What the enemy meant for harm, God turned it for their good and God's glory.

QUESTIONS TO ASK YOURSELF

Here are some questions you must ask yourself:[3]

- Do you feel like you are walking on eggshells in your own home to keep the peace?

- Do you feel like a prisoner in your own home?

- Does your spouse monitor your every move and make you account for every minute?

- Do you ever feel forced to have sex when you don't want to?

- Is your spouse violent with the children, property, or pets?

- Does your spouse call you names or verbally threaten you?

- Do you feel powerless to make your own choices or come and go as you please?

- Does your spouse make all the financial decisions, deny you access to funds, or make you account for every cent?

- Does your spouse humiliate you through actions or words, privately or in front of others?

- Does your spouse frequently accuse you of having affairs?

If you have answered yes to any of these questions, it is likely that you are in an abusive situation. Being abused is frightening and a lonely experience. If you find yourself in the desert of abuse and are asking yourself the question, "Is there something wrong with me, and am I the reason my spouse does this? Am I the only one?" you are walking through a desert place. If you are kept in fear for your physical safety, you can be controlled. If you have experienced verbal, emotional, or physical abuse before, then you know the person is capable of doing it again, which causes a great deal of stress. Abusers are not actually out of control; rather, they are trying to control the victim.

Living this way can make you feel all alone. Getting out of an abusive or violent relationship isn't always easy. You may still be hoping your spouse will change. Even though leaving an abusive situation can be frightening, the risk of staying is far too great. Once someone has used violence against you, it increases the chances of threats and repeated behavior. Abusers have cycles or patterns of behavior.[4]

In Ephesians 5, the Apostle Paul described a godly husband as loving and sacrificial. "Husbands, love your wives, just as Christ loved the church and gave himself up for her," Paul wrote. Christ's love for people was not characterized by overbearing dominance, nor was his leadership characterized by control. Jesus was a meek man as He lived on earth. His leadership was based on selfless love. His leadership was based on thoughtfulness, grace, and sensitivity to others' needs and feelings. He was and still is victorious. *With Jesus, you can choose to be a victor and not a victim.* Learn to live out the life of Christ in your home.

HIDING AND COVERING

When a person walks through abuse, violence, and betrayal to other experiences in life that can leave one feeling like damaged goods, the person learns to operate in a system of hiding and covering. Sometimes we cover for the abuser, and other times we hide behind shame or what others will think if they know what we have experienced. We were protected and covered when we entered this world through our mother's womb. Human beings enter the world with their mothers and yet die as individuals.

Children in nurturing and loving families receive the message that they are lovable, capable, and valuable. This forms a certain buffer of self-esteem. Children that grow up with major dysfunction seem to feel unlovable, defective, and have a sense of incompetence. The outcome of family violence, abuse, and neglect leaves a person feeling like damaged goods. Even when a teacher tells a student he or she will never amount to anything, this leaves a scar that has the ability to destroy life. These children grow up with a failure to thrive, lack of initiative, sleep problems, sleepwalking, eating disorders, shoplifting or stealing, obsessive/

compulsive habits, problems in school, or bedwetting to about the age of twelve.[5]

These teenagers and adults grow up with dependent attitudes, false acceptance of guilt and blame, inability to trust, mistrusting self and others, repressed anger and hostility, depression, boundary issues, control and abuse issues, perfectionism, physical complaints such as headaches, insomnia, chest pain, back pain, sinus problems, immune-support problems as a result of chronic stress or chronic shock, chronic feelings of embarrassment and feeling like they don't measure up, guilt and toxic shame, evasiveness, passivity, sexual isolation or promiscuity, and a whole host of other symptoms. Some experience chronic fatigue, exhaustion, accident proneness, isolation, and a lack of close relationships. While many live with post-traumatic stress disorder from living under too much stress for too long, many never reach their potential in life until they realize they are victors in Jesus and not victims.

I have heard some teenagers resort to piercings for attention due to a lack of a father's love exhibited in the home. These young teenagers are saying that they have never experienced hearing their father say, "I love you." Anyone can resort to covering pain!

People try to cover pain and hide from God just like what happened in the Garden of Eden. Whether you have walked through the desert and feel like damaged goods, or experienced severe violence and abuse at the hand of a parent or spouse, God is still your healer. The cycle of violence and abuse is truly broken in the lives of victims when they realize they don't have to accept or tolerate it anymore and the healing begins. It is truly complete when they feel that what they have gone through is like a bad movie they watched. It almost seems as though it never happened, but it did! Whether you have walked through the desert of damaged goods and feel worthless, or perhaps you tried to cover your pain through many other ways, there is healing found in God's Word.

SHAME AND REJECTION

The enemy uses shame and rejection to try to destroy you. He attempts to cripple you at a young age so you never move forward. When people experience false shame about something that has happened to them, that was no fault of their own, they can live with an evil foreboding that hangs like a dark cloud over their heads. The spirit of rejection comes to set them up to be upset. The enemy will say, "You are worthless" or "No one will ever love you" to get you to throw in the towel to quit!

Never give up! God takes the shame, the pain, and the rejection, and instead He accepts us and heals us. We are accepted in Him when we come to the Father through His Son Jesus! What an amazing journey it will be for you if you will cry out to Him now. He is waiting for you to turn to Him. I promise you that He will heal you and restore you if you will seek Him with your whole heart! No matter what has happened to you, or what you have done, God is still in the healing business. No matter what sin you have committed, God's redemption is still sufficient. No matter what people say, still look to Jesus. Remember, hurting people hurt others. We must all look to Jesus!

CHAPTER 7

SEXUAL SIN AND SEDUCTIONS EXPOSED

Don't Give in to Temptation

Unfortunately, when people step outside the boundaries that God has placed in His Word and choose to have sex with someone, they become one with that person. Whether married or not, we develop a soul tie, and there is a natural drawing to each other. This explains why women who have been married to abusive husbands often take them back repeatedly. This also explains why a person who has experienced date rape is often drawn to the same person again. God never intended for either spouse to abuse each other. He never intended for men or women to abuse one another.

Also, when there have been repeated affairs on the husband's part, the wife will frequently have severe pain and want them back. She is still clinging to the memory of her true love and who the man was prior to his choice to sin. Women who step outside the boundaries of marriage and have affairs can cause their husband to experience the same pain and rejection. When either spouse steps outside of God's plan for sex in marriage, then the spirits enter all. We become one with every partner through sex.

Thank God for His Word and the power of the Name of Jesus that breaks the soul ties when we confess sin and apply the blood to our mind, will, and emotions.

If you have been caught in the trap of seduction through sex outside marriage or perhaps working in a strip club or private men's club, God wants to deliver you now. If you have had numerous sexual partners, you can pray right now:

Father, in the Name of Jesus, I confess my sin (and name each person) of sex with others outside Your will, and I ask You to break the soul ties through the blood of Jesus. Forgive me and cleanse me. I ask You to make me whole and pure through Your blood. Amen.

After you have prayed this prayer, begin to read the book of John in the New Testament and get connected with a ladies' or men's group at a local church. Staying connected produces life and a healthy support system.

If you have never accepted Jesus and been born-again, now is the time! Pray this:

Father, in the Name of Jesus, I confess my sin and ask You to forgive me. Come into my heart and be the Lord of my life.

There is healing in Jesus!

Men, please read Proverbs 5, 6, and 7. There are many valuable words of wisdom that will keep you from destroying your life, marriage, and family. One day of pleasure is not worth ruining the rest of your life. Don't be led astray by a strange woman. Don't be led away by seducing words. Women, don't be the woman that the enemy uses to destroy a marriage and family. It produces death and lifelong consequences that you will regret.

PURITY IN A WORLD GONE MAD

People don't really think about what they are doing when they are led astray by the spirit of lust. They are consumed to the point of addiction.

They are totally blind to the consequences that will happen due to the sin of immorality and adultery. When the spirit of lust takes over, they will ignore their position and will be so deceived they begin to rationalize their wrongs. They burn with lust to sin and move forward with their desire. They are unaware of the deadly consequences that occur and the depression that follows. There are damaged relationships, not only with a spouse, but with children, grandchildren, and extended family. Hearts are damaged and broken.

Song of Solomon speaks of stolen waters being sweet, but only a momentary delight. Sexual addictions and compulsions begin and have only moments of delight that end in destruction. Then the same habits always come next. First the one in sin only thinks of protecting himself or herself. They always blame others and never admit or take responsibility for their actions. Then they always want to destroy all evidence. Hypocrisy follows and then divine judgment.

David and Bathsheba experienced judgment and the death of their child. Murder and all manner of sin followed. Today, nations do the same; it's just called abortion. Lust gives birth to sin. Sin leads to death. Let's look at the book of James. James lets us know the purpose of tests.

The Bible says, "Blessed is the man who endures temptation; for when he has been approved, he will receive the crown of life which the Lord has promised to those who love Him" (James 1:12, NKJV). The Bible also says, "Let no one say when he is tempted, 'I am tempted by God'; for God cannot be tempted by evil, nor does He Himself tempt anyone. But each one is tempted when he is drawn away by his own desires and enticed. Then, when desire has conceived, it gives birth to sin; and sin, when it is full-grown, brings forth death. Do not be deceived, my beloved brethren" (James 1:13–16, NKJV).

In 1 Thessalonians 4 Paul talks about living to please God. He goes on to explain:

> For this is the will of God, even your sanctification, that ye should
> abstain from fornication:
>   That every one of you should know how to possess his vessel in
> sanctification and honour;

Not in the lust of concupiscence, even as the Gentiles which know not God:

That no man go beyond and defraud his brother in any matter: because that the Lord is the avenger of all such, as we also have forewarned you and testified.

For God hath not called us unto uncleanness, but unto holiness.

He therefore that despiseth, despiseth not man, but God, who hath also given unto us his holy Spirit.

But as touching brotherly love ye need not that I write unto you: for ye yourselves are taught of God to love one another.

—1 THESSALONIANS 4:3–9, KJV

To abstain from sexual sin and other sin, the Bible instructs us to:

Walk in the Spirit, and you shall not fulfill the lust of the flesh. For the flesh lusts against the Spirit, and the Spirit against the flesh; and these are contrary to one another, so that you do not do the things that you wish. But if you are led by the Spirit, you are not under the law. Now the works of the flesh are evident, which are: adultery, fornication, uncleanness, lewdness, idolatry, sorcery, hatred, contentions, jealousies, outbursts of wrath, selfish ambitions, dissensions, heresies, envy, murders, drunkenness, revelries, and the like; of which I tell you beforehand, just as I also told *you* in times past, that those who practice such things will not inherit the kingdom of God. But the fruit of the Spirit is love, joy, peace, longsuffering, kindness, goodness, faithfulness, gentleness, self-control. Against such there is no law. And those *who are* Christ's have crucified the flesh with its passions and desires. If we live in the Spirit, let us also walk in the Spirit. Let us not become conceited, provoking one another, envying one another.

—GALATIANS 5:16–26, NKJV

We live in a day where moral standards have faded and what was once considered shameful, disgraceful, and sinful are now practiced widespread throughout the church. Sexual sin is rampant throughout society, both in the church and in the world. Believers sometimes try to justify their actions rather than acknowledging their sin and turning back to God in repentance. When we have a heart change and desire to please our heavenly Father, we repent rather than cover because we know that God sees sin and hates it. We learn to hate what God hates. It is similar to a child who deeply desires to please his or her natural father. God loves people and hates sin.

The way to break the sin habits is to believe in the blood of Jesus and the finished work on the cross. You have to know about the blood of Jesus and truly get born-again. You were born into sin. (Study Psalm 51:1–7.) You have to believe in the blood and learn how to appropriate (or use) the blood on a daily basis. You take your faith and turn it into confession. Then to see the power of God in your life, you have to expect it. Expect great things from God. There is nothing the blood of Jesus cannot accomplish. (See chapter on confession.)

The following contains facts on adultery, fornication, and uncleanness. The sexual sins of adultery, fornication, and uncleanness are at the beginning of Paul's list. The definition of *adultery* is: "voluntary sexual intercourse of a married person with someone other than his or her lawful spouse."[1] The words *adultery* and *fornication* both come from the same Greek word *porneia* which includes all sexual activity outside of marriage. This is inclusive also of homosexuality. The word *porneia* is also fornication and "illicit sexual intercourse."[2] The Bible used the word *porne*, which is listed as "a prostitute, harlot."[3] In God's view, a woman who commits adultery has become a prostitute. People can give a whole host of excuses to explain, but the bottom line is that God views such an act as prostitution. When a woman sets her mind on having a man sexually, whether married or not, she has sinned not only against herself, but also against God. Based on God's Word, sex is only morally correct between a husband and wife.

The word *pornos* denotes "a man who indulges in fornication, a fornicator,"[4] which is also a man who has had sex outside the realm of marriage. Even though his mind, will, and emotions may lure him to think he has found his dream girl, the Greek word *porneia* means he has slept with a prostitute. No matter what we think as a society, this is God's view.

Whenever a man steps outside the boundaries of marriage or has sex with a woman who is not his wife, God calls this the same as having sex with a prostitute, and it is merely for instant gratification, which is cheap and dirty. When a person obsesses in his or her mind, there is a great chance he or she will eventually act on the thought. This is why it is so important to renew your mind in the Word of God. (See chapter containing "Confessing God's Word.")

The word *pornography* also comes from the Greek word *pornos* and from the word *grapho*, which means "to write." This explains pornography that is rampant across society. *Pornography* means "obscene literature, art, or photography"[5] (Greek *pornograph(os)*: "writing or writer about harlots"). The word *fornication* means "voluntary sexual intercourse between two unmarried persons."[6] The word *unclean* means "not clean; dirty, morally impure; evil; vile: an unclean attitude."[7] Ask yourself this question: Has Satan lured you or someone you know into pornography or unclean ideas that led to adultery? Has the enemy been attacking your mind with unclean, impure, or dirty thoughts? This is how the enemy of your soul starts to lure you away to sin. If you dwell on wrong thoughts, Satan can build a stronghold of uncleanness to lead you into actions that can destroy your life, family, career, and destiny.

The man or woman who burns with lust and visualizes sex with a partner is just waiting to act on it. When the spirit enters, it brings addiction and compulsion. You must crucify the flesh daily and renew your mind in the Word of God. God always provides a way of escape. *Most importantly, God loves the sinner but hates the sin.*

Scripture signifies that sexual purity is attainable. We must learn to cultivate habits of holiness. Today, just as in Greece during the first century, sin is still rampant. If God tells us to do something, He equips us to be able to do so. Purity is a matter of the heart.

You can lust for sex, power, money, position, or things. Anything that draws you away from God is idolatry and sin. Sin brings death. Purity of heart opens your eyes to see God and His hand in everything. Purity of heart creates an inner desire to please God, our heavenly Father, and to know Him above all else. Choose to honor God and live a life of purity.

There are ways to cultivate purity in marriage. My husband and I have boundaries that might seem a little strong. My husband will not meet another woman for a meal, even in business, unless I am present. He always makes sure others are present in a group setting. In most cases, when he travels for business, he always takes me with him. We choose to protect our marriage. I don't have a meal with the opposite sex unless my husband is present. We have close friends, but there are things you share that are only for your spouse.

Cultivate a relationship that provides protection. Always think about how your situation may appear. Avoid the appearance of evil. Never put yourself in a position to be tempted and destroyed. Choose to put yourself in a position of blessing by honoring and obeying God's Word. Choose to honor God, honor God's Word, and honor your spouse. You will be thankful! Let's take a look at how things can go wrong very quickly without proper boundaries and established honor.

ANGELA'S AFFAIR

Angela got married at a young age and was happy with Kenny. They tried to have children but to no avail. She gained weight through covering her pain in excessive eating and decided years later to lose the weight. After Angela became thinner, she began to see that other men seemed to notice her, and she lost interest in Kenny, the husband of her youth. She became more interested in going out with her friends after work than spending time with her husband.

She started thinking, "Kenny is not good enough for me" and began to have a soured opinion of him. He began to complain of her lack of affection and wondered if she was having an affair. He began to fear losing her because of the changes in her since her exercise program.

People get angry, defensive, and touchy when they are walking away from God's plan. They carry guilt, so therefore, they have something to hide. Hidden sin produces anger and guilt. The Bible tells us in 1 John 1:9 when we confess our sin, God is faithful and just to forgive us. Willfully choosing to walk away from God leads to spiritual death.

These are some of the classic symptoms where the enemy comes in to bring destruction in your home, marriage, and family one little step at a time. He does not announce, "I am here to destroy your life," but he subtly and strategically carries out a plot of your demise.

When we have our focus on Jesus rather than on ourselves or how we appear to others, we know that we desire more than anything else to please our heavenly Father. His opinion matters most.

Chapter 8

SEASONS IN LIFE

To Love and Honor

Marriages go through seasons in life. We must pay attention and stay connected to our spouse to thrive. Love is a commitment. Love always sees the best in each other. Love always covers. Love never fails. When we truly surrender our lives physically and emotionally to God, we can learn to walk in victory under every attack and plan of the enemy. Choose to always honor your spouse. Honor builds up and dishonor destroys. The definition of *honor* is "to value, respect, or highly esteem; to treat as precious, weighty, or valuable."[1] *Dishonor* is "to treat as common or ordinary."[2]

When a husband asks his wife to forgive him, and truly means it with all sincerity, he is giving her a precious gift of love. A wife wants to be honored by her husband. Sometimes the more negative her words may sound, the more she is actually seeking positive affirmation and love. Speak highly of each other in front of your children and others. Don't dare look lustfully at other people. Keep each other informed of plans and always keep commitments.

When a husband speaks words that sound and feel unloving and disrespectful, he is simply planting seeds of doubt about what is in his heart toward her. A man full of wisdom learns to hear what his wife is actually saying rather than getting angry and lashing back or stonewalling her with silence. Don't wait until your spouse dies or you lose him or her to recognize how little you expressed your love and adoration. Learn to look at your spouse and see him or her as a treasure God has given you. God created women to be honored and respected. Learn to treasure her! You can begin by saying "thank you" to your spouse.

A man gains God's favor when he submits to his wife's needs for love and understanding, as well as loyalty and honor. Be faithful, no matter if you still feel butterflies of love or are in a dry season where it feels like the love is a little stagnant. Communicate your love by your actions.

A man knows that if his wife respects him in her heart, she will in turn communicate that same respect. Men value your love more than words can adequately express, but they still need respect. A man doesn't always deserve respect, but in order for him to hear his wife's heart, a wife must choose to offer him respect. Call or send him a text thanking him for being a wonderful husband out of the clear blue. Love your spouse as if you were doing it as unto the Lord.

If you are in a cold season where there seems to be silence, start doing the same things you used to do when dating. If you are in the springtime and new life is budding, cherish and honor the time. If you are in a fall season when things are being pruned, learn to walk in love and respect each other as well. Love is not just a feeling. It is a commitment. If you just got married and are in a summer month, where all seems grand, cherish the hot nights and long walks together. There are seasons in life and marriage. Don't allow your eyes to stray. When people begin to stray, the enemy plants a seed of doubt that causes people to reason. Reasoning produces bad feelings that produce negative actions.

The grass may appear greener on the other side of the street, but there is just more fertilizer in their yard. Don't believe the lies of the enemy. Always speak the truth in love. Lying opens the door to the enemy. If we choose to give the devil a crack, he will swing the door right off its hinges to come in and destroy our lives. He is evil and is out to destroy life. There are always two plans. You must carefully choose God's plan. If it doesn't line up with God's Word, it is sin. Anything you have to lie about or be secretive about is sin.

If you have not left your parents emotionally, physically, financially or spiritually, you will not be successful in these areas. If you choose your friends or your work over spouse and family, you are walking away from God. If you choose your kids over your spouse, you are walking away from God as well. I am not talking about proper care of your children, but I am stressing that God has order in families. God has order that produces righteousness and life. We must learn God's ways and apply them to our lives if we want to succeed. Before it's too late for you, run to God and His Word for all the answers. He cares for you.

CHAPTER 9

THE PATH OF RESTLESSNESS

Don't Give in to Despair

While men used to be the primary bread winners, today we have many women in this role. The role of financial provider brings an added responsibility and stress that women are somewhat unaware of, unless they are the main income earner. Women think men are busy, while men think the same thing about women. We get used to the fast pace in life and get used to always being busy, like it is something to brag about or receive an award, when in reality it is a life that is futile. Busyness leads to emptiness. Emptiness leads to despair.

We learn to walk alone with God, even in our busy days, when we learn to trust Him with our daily life. In Psalm 18, when David cried out to the Lord to be rescued from his enemies, this is how God responded: "He opened the heavens and came down; dark storm clouds were beneath his feet. Mounted on a mighty angelic being, he flew, soaring on the wings of the wind. He shrouded himself in darkness, veiling his approach with dark rain clouds. Thick clouds shielded the brightness around him and rained down hail and burning coals. The LORD thundered from heaven; the voice of the Most High resounded amid the hail and burning coals. He shot his arrows and scattered his enemies; his lightning flashed, and they were greatly confused" (Psalm 18: 9–11, 13–14, NLT).

The picture David gave us is one of God as a Mighty Warrior set on rescuing His own (that is us, my friend). Then we see the portrayal soften as God turns His focus from David's enemies to rescuing David. God loves to restore and rescue His own. He wants to rescue you too! "He reached down from heaven and rescued me; he drew me out of deep waters...He led me to a place of safety; he rescued me because he delights in me" (Psalm 18:16, 19, NLT). God rescued David from his enemies by bringing him out into a spacious place or a place of safety. He draws us out of deep waters. God wants to rescue us!

I remember personally going to Christian counseling many years ago after walking through marital abuse and divorce. The female counselor advised me to buy the book *Men Who Hate Women & The Women Who Love Them*. On my drive home I stopped by a local bookstore to pick up the recommended book. As I was searching the shelves, a book on family violence seem to supernaturally light up and was illuminated to me as it fell off a shelf. I can't really explain it; either an angel of the Lord knocked it off to get my attention or it was closer to the edge than it should have been. Needless to say, it certainly got my attention.

I remember reading the pages with tears streaming down my face in pain. I knew that the God of the universe was exhibiting His love for me and wanted me to understand what had been happening to me. I still stand in amazement at the goodness of the Lord to bring me understanding through this book. It seemed as if the Lord Himself began to teach me, heal me, and bring understanding about things I did not understand. You may be reading this now and be in a similar place; or you may be totally distracted in some other area.

Is your life distracted by many things, heavy laden with the cares of this world and the recent wilderness you might find yourself in? Are you weary from being busy and hearing all the reports of friends with cancer and the recent job losses? Are you weary due to being abandoned by your spouse of many years? Are you stressed out due to a business situation that left you holding massive debt? Do you constantly feel a pressure to work harder, do more, achieve more, only to find yourself exhausted at the end of another day? Perhaps you even find yourself in a place of delight with the new grandchildren, but also find yourself trying to do too much for your children as well.

Perhaps you, too, need to be rescued by the *God of rest*, who is also longing to bring you into a spacious place and draw you out of deep and troubling waters. That place might be an overdue vacation or getaway. Other times it is a cancelled trip or a sudden loss in family that gives us time away from the daily distractions and noise of life. God gave us a time of rest when we had the privilege and gift of time to spend the last seventeen days of Daddy's life with him in the cancer center. We were removed from the everyday concerns and were focused on Daddy. That is what God wants too. He wants us to focus on Him as our Daddy. He is our heavenly Father!

You might find yourself in a spacious place now and just don't realize it yet. This is the place where we find Him. You might be out of work and have the God-given opportunity to spend more time with your children for a season and spend more time in God's Word. You might be on a trip and get snowed in to be quiet and get rest. He rescues us because He delights in us. He longs to spend time with His beloved. That is you and me!

When a man loses his job he feels worthless. When a man walks out on his wife and family, it leaves a trail of rejection, abandonment, anger, despair, worry, fear, and a sense of hopelessness. The enemy of our soul uses this to reinforce any loss of our sense of value and worth, which are two things all people need.

One thing I want to mention here is that whatever we sow is what we reap. (See Galatians 6:7.) If a woman is dating a married man, what makes you think she will be loyal to anyone? A man that will go out with a married woman is the same thing. People sometimes think they want something they can't have. Other times, it is the "chase and conquer" syndrome or what I like to call the "Romeo and Juliet" syndrome. Either of these is a path of drama and chaos.

When we know who we are in Christ, we can remain calm even in the midst of storms. However, it takes intense training in the midst of a storm to get to the place of complete trust in God. Our emotions want to run wild during these times of crisis. The only way to learn to walk in the Spirit of God and be ruled by your spirit is through training. Whatever you train becomes stronger. Even when you work out for a few weeks, you will begin to notice a difference in your body and energy. The same thing happens when we train our mind by renewal in the Word of God. Listening to sermons, scriptures, reading the Word, meditating on the Word, and praying are all vital components of renewing the mind. This intense training equips us to live above crazy makers and the attempts of Satan to throw us into a tailspin with our emotions running wild.

After abandonment, not only is a woman left with solely taking care of the children, if any, but also the maintenance of the home and financial responsibility which creates extreme pressure for a season. Men also find themselves in heartache and pain, as well as shock when a wife abandons her husband and family. These are places where we can become restless and live in fear. Life has a tendency to produce stress. We can enter into bondage to fear, worry, anxiety, and a whole host of negative emotions. The Bible tells us Jesus came to "deliver them who through fear of death were all their lifetime subject to bondage" (Hebrews 2:15, KJV). God wants us to trust Him. God wants us to rest in Him.

God desires that we learn to trust Him whether we are single, married, or about to walk down the aisle on our wedding day. You may be feeling all alone for many reasons and are wondering if God is ever going to move on your behalf. You may be happily married and lost the sparkle in your marriage or the twinkle in your eye for your mate. You may feel like the world is caving in due to inability to pay your bills. No matter where you are, God is still faithful. He uses our desert experiences to purge us from sin and self so we reach the place of trusting Him, above all else. He promises to turn everything out for our good and His glory. He desires that we learn to rest in Him. He desires that we learn to rest in His provision, His care, and just learn to enjoy spending time in His presence. You are a *priceless treasure* to Him!

CHAPTER 10

LOVESICKNESS

Communicate Love with Actions

Have you ever felt butterflies or had cold clammy hands when you met someone and gazed into their eyes? Do you enjoy spending time with your spouse? Do you ever just sit and talk? When was the last time you actually talked with your spouse? Do you come home and sit down in front of a television, or do you actually talk and listen to your spouse? In all relationships, it is vital to have good communication. We must continue to work on it whether we have just gotten engaged or have been married for thirty years.

God lets us know we are one with Him. An example is when my husband called on his drive to work to share something he heard on the radio from Song of Solomon. I happened to be studying the same thing. See how we were one with God—a healthy love. Are you lovesick or love healthy? (See Song of Solomon 2:5.)

Let's look at the communication between couples within Song of Solomon. Courtship, wedding, and marriage are all portrayed in the verses. Solomon speaks first and then Shulamite, though it may be hard to follow which one is speaking. It begins with the engaged couple building a strong and loving relationship together. Both understand the importance of words.

They seem to be having a competition going on of who can compliment the most and out-praise each other.

The Bible says, "How beautiful you are, my darling, how beautiful! Your eyes are like doves" (Song of Solomon 1:15, NLT). Solomon's comparison is greater than physical attraction by comparing Shulamite's eyes to a dove. Our eyes are the windows to our soul. They strongly communicate more than our words, and are more honest. Solomon not only saw her outward beauty, but her inward beauty as well. Even when they are married and still in love, we continue to see Solomon talking about the gaze in Shulamite's eyes (Song of Solomon 4:9). Can you say with your eyes to your mate, you are still in love? Perhaps this is why there is a huge selection of makeup for the eyes in stores across the nations. When makeup is properly applied, it complements the face and the eyes are highlighted with shadow, liner and mascara.

Solomon and Shulamite continue to affirm their love for each other. Solomon praises the sensuality of her eyes while Shulamite praises him for his charm by referring to Solomon as being pleasant. Together, they admire their marriage bed and home. This proves our words are vital to our love life. The verbal exchanges change from "I" to "our." This is turning point in any marriage when you start to think about life together. It's called becoming one!

Solomon is the king of Israel. Shulamite praises him not only for their intimate bed, but also for his amazing provision in their home. She described the home with cedar beams, and it makes her feel safe as she affirms Solomon's thoughtfulness.

He took her from her home town to the palace, and she says "I am the rose of Sharon"—meaning she is like a wild flower in the palace. She is likening herself to a beautiful white blossom, referring to herself as a flower in the meadow. This affirmation corresponds to the feelings of doubt and low self-worth she is experiencing of being capable to live in the palace, even though Solomon has given her a place of comfort and security.

In chapter 2, Solomon describes her as a lily among the thorns. He tells her she may be a wild flower, but she is his wild flower and makes all others look like thorns. Solomon is expressing his admiration and letting her know she is the only one in his eyes. She is unique among all the women. He keeps affirming his devotion to her. Shulamite affirms her admiration of Solomon. This is vitally important in your relationship today.

In the 117 verses of Song of Solomon, Shulamite speaks more than Solomon. Women talk the most—big surprise! Nothing has changed in life. Shulamite may talk more than Solomon, but he chooses his words very carefully. Both dedicate their words to expressing how important they are to each other. Shulamite is at ease and relaxed in his presence. Are you at ease in the presence of your husband? Husbands, is your wife at ease in your presence?

The culture we live in today is operating at such a fast pace and is a society of comparison; from our dress to our notoriety, in everything we do and whatever circle we find ourselves, there is the potential for jealousy. Solomon and Shulamite go overboard to let each other know they are number one in each other's eyes. Only if couples would do that today!

God says marriage is holy matrimony. It is set apart to God and not just a human institution. If we don't have God as the head in our marriage, it can seem like an institution. We are set apart to one another as well. We are holy to each other and set apart to God together. Make sure your spouse knows there is no one else in the circle and that he or she occupies the unique place in your eyes for the success of your marriage.

In the fast pace that society has reached, with all sorts of time-saving gadgets, to the latest technology, the stress of life puts added pressure on marriage and family. Today, like never before, we see marriages ending in divorce.

What caused the love healthy relationship to become sick? How did the relationship start out? Did it begin with the physical, or did it start with friendship? Society changes and media have crept into the homes and families across the globe. Magazines show women with perfect faces and thin bodies that present an image that not everyone is able to attain. God created us all as individuals in all shapes and sizes.

The speed of technology that was supposed to save us time has only given us the capability of moving faster and created stress through the pressure of unrealistic expectations. I don't think Jesus moved at this "breakneck" speed. As a matter of fact, Lazarus died and lay in the grave for four days before Jesus showed up and raised him up from the dead. He took time to touch the people and connect with them. He communicated with them. When we are in such a hurry to move to the next person, we don't touch the people we are with at present.

It's like the gal we saw today with summer garments on in the middle of winter with the temperature below 40 degrees. She had sandals on and was running through the parking lot. She was dressed for summer.

Marketplaces do it also. They have all the latest fashions out for the next season before we are even in the beginning of the one at present. The world is rushing to the next season, the next greatest fad, the next greatest technical gizmo, the next love affair, the next greatest sports game. What is the world coming to at this breakneck speed of going nowhere?

We communicate by our actions that we do not enjoy where we are at present. The same can happen with your spouse. When you aren't really listening with your heart to what your spouse is saying, you are communicating to them they are unimportant. Racing to answer your phone to make sure you don't miss a new text or email is a communication signal that the people you are spending time with are not as important as the people at a distance. Are you seeing the trend? It seems we are at a similar place as the Garden of Eden and the Tree of Knowledge. People get caught up in knowledge and technology rather than relationship. And we wonder what has happened to this current generation. God have mercy!

Good communication is imperative for a healthy relationship with your family and children. Children enjoy the laughter around the evening dinner table and the goodnight hug or kiss when you tuck them into bed. Most importantly, good communication is one of the most vital ingredients of a healthy marriage. Enjoying spending time with your spouse is another sign. When you love to just "be" with your spouse, no matter what you are doing, it is evidence of a healthy marriage. Enjoying time together and having casual conversation about each other's day is also vital. The casual time around the dinner table laughing and discussing daily events, and the early morning hug and kiss with your spouse out the door are signs of a healthy relationship. Also, being able to feel free to discuss anything with your spouse is vital to a healthy relationship. This is a clear sign of a safe harbor or safe place to be transparent with your spouse. Showing public affection is also a definite sign.

Loss of interest in each other and lack of conversation that resorts to withdrawing and a cold atmosphere are signs of an unhealthy relationship. You can turn your relationship around by working on it. Keeping secrets and developing emotional relationships outside of marriage is a huge danger. No one should enter into an intimate conversation with coworkers or casual friends of the opposite sex when married. The enemy sets us up to be destroyed. Remember, all relationships require work to maintain them.

We can begin to feel alone in the world with all technology and no real face-to-face communication. I believe this is another trap of the enemy to stop and shut down vital communication skills that develop and maintain relationships. We can begin to feel the lingering toll of stress if we don't double up on our time spent with the Lord in prayer and reading the Bible. The more we pour out, the more we need to take in. It's similar to exercising. The harder you exercise the more intake of food your body requires to remain healthy. It is the same with relationships that last.

Don't move from butterflies to loss of relationship. Cherish and guard your relationship with your spouse. Set boundaries and keep your heart healthy toward your spouse. Don't allow the enemy to get one open door to cause you to stumble. Guard your heart, guard your relationships, and guard your family.

CHAPTER 11

STUMBLING IN THE DARK

*When we don't choose to guard our own
heart, we are prone to stumble.*

Someone very dear to my heart is currently walking through what appears to be the darkest days in her life. Her husband walked out of their marriage, leaving her and the two kids behind. Not to mention, he left for another woman. What made it harder to understand was the fact the other woman was a relative. The rejection that comes from such bad choices leaves the wife feeling despair and financial stress; the children are left with knowing their father lied, ran off with a relative, and left an unfit picture of the representation of a father.

Unfortunately, since we primarily ascertain our picture of our heavenly Father based on what we experience from our earthly father, we can have a wrong perception and image of God based on our circumstances.

God loves us so much that He sent His Only Son to redeem us back to Himself. Unfortunately, here on earth, people make really bad choices and leave the fallout of consequences to the children and their spouse. People that make these kinds of choices are blinded by the enemy and selfish. They have lost their way.

It is during these times that we feel we are *stumbling in the dark* just to make it through another day. The overwhelming feelings of hopelessness one minute, to anger and despair the next, can be a heavy weight on the emotions and damage the soul. It is during these times that we must run to our heavenly Father and seek Him with our whole heart. He is close to the brokenhearted.

God still loves the father and husband who ran off, but God hates his sin. There is forgiveness for him if and when he repents. God even loves the woman he left his wife for as well.

Unfortunately, many men and women both, get in the cycle of having affairs and committing adultery. This damages your soul. The volcanic fallout that is left behind from these horrible choices can leave lifelong devastation to the rest of the family. The enemy will try to make you think no one has ever made it through this before and that no one truly understands. The truth is you can be surrounded by many people and still feel all alone. (Read Proverbs 1–7.)

GOD'S SECRET

Through the death of a spouse, the death of a father or mother, the death of a marriage through separation and divorce, the loss of a child or the many disappointments in life that can leave us feeling hopeless and barren, we can still have hope in our eyes when we know this man Jesus! He is the secret to joy in our lives when we are walking through the wilderness or our own personal desert of circumstances. Life is sometimes just not fair.

What God wants us to learn and come to know is Him, even in the midst of our darkest hour and desert. It is in the wilderness or desert that we truly come to know Him as Lord and Savior. The secret that God wants us to learn is to come to Him, embrace Him, and wait upon Him because He is our deliverer. It is in the darkest times of our lives that we grow closer to God and realize just who He is in our lives. (Read Exodus 14:13–14.) Blessings begin to flow when we fall in love with the Lord and learn to obey His Word.

CHAPTER 12

OBEDIENCE AND BLESSING

Knowing Him as Lord

I f I could just touch the hem of His garment, I could be made whole. If I could just feel His touch on my face and know He is right beside me, I know I could make it. It is in these times of desperation that we come to know Him beyond all measure. If I can just press my way through this crazy situation and madness then I know I could make it another day. He is right beside us and has never left. The times of loneliness, where we sit contemplating our life and removed from the distractions of other people, could be the most advantageous times we have to be in the right mindset to actually listen and hear what God is trying to speak to us.

When God gives us hope, the enemy tries to get us to dwell on the negative rather than the positive hope that God gave us through His Word or encouragement through a total stranger. It is when God changes the entire order of a church service just for you to let you know how important you are to Him. It is in these times that we find refreshing and His love rushing in to calm our soul. He likes to amaze us with His love. He is so amazing! There are no words to adequately describe His love.

How many times have you had the Lord gently whisper to you, but you ignored Him by bringing people and noise into the circumstance so you would not be silent? How many times do you remember God tugging at the door of your heart to come away and spend some alone time with Him? Do you find a reason to resist? We sometimes struggle with being alone in order to touch the hem of His garment so we can be made whole. We miss the blessings He desires to give us when we run from Him.

When we finally settle down and listen to what God is saying, we find the refreshing, the blessing, and the stillness to know God is in control. We learn to trust Him after we have touched the hem of His garment.

OBEDIENCE BRINGS BLESSING

The Bible tells us that all things work out for our good and His glory. (See Romans 8:28.) You might be in the middle of your own personal struggle right now and don't feel that way at present. You may have been abandoned and are feeling all alone. You might be the one who walked out on your mate and left your spouse and kids. Either way, when we repent, God promises to forgive and restore. Repentance is produced by godly sorrow. Just being caught in an act of sin is not godly sorrow. (See 1 John 1:9.)

God says in His Word to us, "I know the plans I have for you...plans to prosper you and not to harm you, plans to give you hope and a future" (Jeremiah 29:11, NIV). Why does God have these plans for us? What corresponding action or response is required of us? What is God hoping we will do in response to His promise?

He tells us why He intends good for us: "Then you will call on me and come and pray to me, and I will listen to you. You will seek me and find me when you seek me with all your heart. I will be found by you...and will bring you back from captivity" (Jeremiah 29:12–14, NIV).

God not only has great plans for us, but also He desires that we actually live them out in the natural. The Bible says, "For we are of God's making, created in union with the Messiah Yeshua for a life of good actions already prepared by God for us to do" (Ephesians 2:10, CJB). This assures me that I will make it through my season of wilderness and struggles to the other side. God isn't out to destroy me. He wants me to succeed and live an abundant life. He wants us to live out His perfect will and plan for our lives. The vital key here is that it is *His* plan and not ours. "Many are the plans in a man's heart, but it is the Lord's purpose that prevails" (Proverbs 19:21, WYC).

God is speaking to you and to me today! He leads us through His Word and His voice to His perfect plan, His will, and His purpose for each of our lives. Whether you turn to the right or to the left, your ears will hear a voice behind you, saying, "This is the way; walk in it" (Isaiah 30:21).

Are you listening? Do you want to hear what He is speaking to you? Have you surrounded yourself with so many distractions that you don't know Him? As you continue to seek Him, even during the darkest times of your life, He will carry you through, as you trust Him. The Bible says, "...He Who began a good work in you will continue until the day of Jesus Christ [right up to the time of His return], developing [that good work] and perfecting and bringing it to full completion in you" (Philippians 1:6, AMP).

Obedience is the seed for divine favor with God and favor with man. When we honor God we have respect for His Word, His opinions, instructions, and His plan for our lives. God honors those who fear Him. Fear is holy reverence, a sense of awe, and respect. God honors us when we honor Him through church attendance, tithing, and prayer. Prayerlessness is probably the greatest sin for a Christian. If you are not obeying God's Word, you don't love Him. Jesus told us in His Word that those who love Him will obey His Word! When we come to know Him as Lord, we have a desire to obey.

KNOWING HIM AS LORD

Do you know Jesus as Lord, or is He a stranger? Most people meet him while going through a crisis, during a separation and divorce, or during the loss of loved ones. Others come to know Him through tragic loss or the loss of a life career. Do you know Him? Are you afraid to be alone with Him? When you travel, are you able to spend time alone with Him, or must you have someone to meet to feel complete? You will know that you have come to know Him when you can truly be alone with Him. God uses our desert places to teach us important things rather than leaving us there alone. He is with us through the darkest times, even when it seems no one else is present. It is in the valley of despair, or the desert of desertion, where most come to really know Him intimately.

God wants us to truly know (*yada* in Greek) Him as Lord. This means we have to come to a place of rest in Him, trust Him, embrace Him, and love Him with adoration that is unable to be adequately expressed by any human language. It is a place of peace, because He is peace.

HOW DO I GET THERE?

Most people experience their first encounter through a place of desperation. While some are raised in church their entire life and come to know Him at an earlier age, others come to know Him at a well of worship. It is when we come to our deepest place or our well of loneliness that we come to know and worship Him.

What about you? Do you struggle with being alone with Him? Are you married and feeling alone, even with a mate? Are you desiring to be married or perhaps desiring to have a career that has been a dream for years? Are you trying to have a child and find yourself barren? Are you struggling with not feeling emotionally connected with your spouse? Do you sense you are losing your children to adulthood and now you are secretly wishing you had not stayed at home to raise your kids? Do you feel like God has deserted you in the midst of a financial storm when you tithed and did everything you knew to do? Do you sometimes wish you had stayed single because of the emotional outbursts from an angry spouse?

Whatever your well of loneliness, God will meet you there. It is usually difficult to think something good can happen when we are currently experiencing a season of problems or pain. God seems to surprise us at our lowest point with His plans and blessings in our lives.

FOCUS ON JESUS

For the word of God is living and active. Sharper than any double-edged sword, it penetrates even to dividing soul and spirit, joints and marrow; it judges the thoughts and attitudes of the heart.

—HEBREWS 4:12, NIV

How many times have you shared your shattered dreams and the circumstances surrounding your most difficult season in which you now find yourself? You either wind up feeling emotionally drained or angry beyond belief, getting yourself and others all riled up with the emotional distress of the situation. You feel physically weak and sick to the point of either not wanting to eat or overeating to cover your pain. Does either of these fit you? Perhaps you began to focus on yourself and started exercising beyond the normal standard and now find yourself looking in the mirror at this emaciated rail of a human who used to be vibrant and glowing. Women, especially, can fall into despair with the volcanic fallout from emotional devastation due to severe loss or traumatic events. The same can happen to men as well.

Perhaps you are the one who made the wrong choice and now find yourself in the painful consequences. If you choose to ignore the sin, your heart can become calloused and you wander through life from one bad choice to another. When we repent, God is faithful and just to forgive us (1 John 1:9).

CONFESSING THE TRUTH OF GOD'S WORD

When we wander and continue to make bad choices, we have not surrendered some area of our life to God. One of the reasons this happens is because we confess our sin without ever confessing the *truth of God's Word* where we find access to restoration and peace.

His Word empowers us as we speak it. He is able to work from the inside out to change us as we confess His Word over our lives and circumstances.

Your confession shows you are choosing to be in agreement with God, but also in agreement with God about who you are in Christ. When you choose to believe God at His very Word, and begin to declare what He says about you, then you will begin to sense an overwhelming sense of peace and fullness of joy. This is the secret to total restoration of your life.

We learn to magnify God and His Word over our circumstances. When we magnify the Word of God, His Word begins to produce results in our lives. We must choose to love genuinely, live with a heart of forgiveness, choose to walk in humility, and give generously. When we live in this manner, the favor of God is released in our life. The Bible says, "And Jesus grew in wisdom and stature, and in favor with God and men" (Luke 2:52). If the son of God had to grow in these areas, we do too!

If you have a baby that is not growing, you know something is very wrong. If you are a Christian and not growing, you have something spiritually wrong. We must learn to imitate Jesus for real change. God's plan is for each of us to become like Jesus. We are created in His image. When we get the Word of God from our head to our hearts, change will begin to occur.

We then are moved with compassion and constrained by the love of God to do what God says in His Word! We have a desire to give to the kingdom of God here and now, and we choose to walk in love with people. We begin to see people and situations through the eyes of God. We hear what He has to say about people and situations and have the Father's heart for people.

If you do not love people, you do not love God! Check out your own heart! Are you suspicious of people, or do you see the best in everyone? Do you have a desire to lead people to Christ in freedom? Do you desire to constantly experience change in your own life to become more like Christ?

Real and lasting change occurs from the inside out. The Bible says, "Be made new in the attitude of your mind" (Ephesians 4:23, NIV) and "Be transformed by the renewing of your mind" (Romans 12:2, NIV). God is showing us that every behavior starts with a thought. If you want to change the way you act, then you have to change the way you think. You do this by confessing your faith in God because His Word empowers you to think differently about yourself, your situation, and your sin. You learn to conquer your mind with your mouth. Stay in agreement with what God says about you. It is a constant reminder that God is at work within you and for you.

Stay in agreement with God's Word. Read the Bible. Learn from the lessons in Matthew where Jesus was led into the wilderness. Quality leaders are prepared in the wilderness. Jesus was led by the Holy Spirit into the wilderness right after His baptism by John. God the Father said He was well pleased with His Son.

During the wilderness or desert experiences, our personal motives are purified, we become stronger in God and are equipped with boldness, and we learn to understand the necessary transformation for our divine purpose. The greater the call on a person's life, the greater the preparation is necessary.

Jesus was tempted by the "lust of the flesh" to be self-sufficient. He had fasted for forty days and was hungry. This was a need. Jesus said, "It is written, 'Man shall not live by bread alone, but by every word that proceeds from the mouth of God'" (Matthew 4:4, NKJV). Jesus did not become controlling or angry, nor did he rail against Satan. He trusted God!

Jesus was tempted by the "lust of the eyes" to throw himself down since He was the Son of God. Jesus refused to trust Himself. He didn't perform. He knew who He was and who His Father was as well. He stayed in alignment with His Father's will (Matthew 4:5, NKJV). The Bible clearly shows us again that Jesus said, "It is written again, You shall not tempt the LORD your God" (Matthew 4:7, NKJV).

Jesus was also tempted by the "lust of pride" or to be powerful. Jesus refused to take a shortcut that was offered by the enemy to gain power. He already had the power and knew who He was in His Father (Matthew 4:8, NKJV). For the third time, the Bible shows us the principle of quoting the Word of God as a sword against the enemy. Jesus said, "For it is written, 'You shall worship the LORD your God, and Him only you shall serve'" (Matthew 4:10, NKJV).

How do you choose to deal with temptation? If you will choose to use Jesus's method of combating temptation, you will not lose. Jesus never lost. God will give you a scripture for your specific situation. Begin to confess it out of your mouth daily! Declare "It is written" and the words God gives you from the Bible!

When you choose to start responding out of faith in God rather than reacting out of your emotions, you will recognize that you are no longer focused on what happened to you or what you did. You will see you are now focusing on Jesus and choosing to believe that He has a greater plan for your life, even in the most difficult seasons.

It was the same for Peter when He kept his eyes on Jesus. He began to walk on the water. In my personal alone time with God today, the Lord spoke to my heart that no matter what personal struggles you may be experiencing, whether it be the loss of a business, separation and divorce, the loss of a loved one or perhaps, even struggles in your own emotions, never give up. I don't know personally what you are experiencing, but what I do know is that God is faithful when we move toward Him and move forward with corresponding actions to His promises in His Word!

When we feel like giving up and throwing in the towel, that is the time the enemy knows the horizon is in sight and the blessing from God. I am encouraging you NOT to give up! When I step out to share the gift of salvation that is a free gift from God, some hear the message, some receive it in their heart, some scoff, and some just walk away; but the Lord reminds us in His Word to wipe the dust off our feet and move onto the next group of people.

It is the same way in business. God says in His Word that He will prosper whatever we put our hands to—and that is our corresponding action to His instructions. Think of Abraham Lincoln and many other great leaders. Where would they have been if they had given up every time they failed? They kept getting up and moving forward. Look at Peter who walked on the water when he kept His eyes on Jesus. It was not until Peter began to notice the wind and waves of his circumstances that he began to sink. Peter cried out saying, "Lord, save me" (Matthew 14:30). Immediately, Jesus helped him and spoke to him about doubt.

Jesus called out to him and helped him up. Jesus is still calling out today! He wants to help you out of the pit of despair. He is right beside you as you walk through this lonely road of abandonment, or extreme pain from life's circumstances. Get up, get out, and move onto the next group of people. No matter how many people have spoken negatively to you, God has people waiting to bring encouragement. Get moving! All things are possible with God. Keep your focus on Jesus.

GOD SPEAKS

One way God speaks to His children is by asking them questions. When we read the Bible, we see Him doing this throughout both the Old and New Testaments. When Elijah was hiding in the cave, the Lord asked, "Elijah, what are you doing here?" (1 Kings 19:9). When Peter began walking on the water toward Jesus, but turned his focus from Jesus to the wind and waves and began to sink, Jesus asked him, "Why did you not believe?" (Matthew 14:31). When Saul, soon to become Paul, was on the road to Damascus, Jesus asked him, "Why do you persecute me?" (Acts 22:7).

I have already mentioned Hagar and the Woman at the Well in Samaria. "....The angel of God called to Hagar from heaven and said to her, "What's the matter, Hagar?" God has not changed. He is still asking questions today. God still uses questions to get to the heart of any matter and to bring the motive to the surface. Remember in the book of Job, God asked him many questions. They brought truth to light. When we abide in Christ and have proper heart motives, we operate in the light of the Truth of God's Word. When we develop pride and have a haughty attitude with wrong motives, we are in the dark. Which are you currently in: A (abiding) M (motives pure), or are you in P (pride) M (motives impure)? You are either in a.m. or p.m., like it or not. You choose to walk in the light of God's Word or in the darkness of the enemy. When we choose our way saying things like "It's my life" or "It's my business," we are choosing to operate in pride and darkness.

When we choose to walk in the light and truth of God's Word, we stay under God's protection. When we choose to go our own way and have wrong motives, we live in darkness and despair. We stay in the desert until we learn the lesson. When we stay in truth, we live and have peace because we are not living in secret. When we are in sin, we become defensive and angry. These are symptoms of sin.

DOES GOD HAVE THE ANSWERS?

When we find ourselves in a desert of sin or through the sin of someone close to us, we might wonder, "Does God have the answers?" The answer is a resounding yes! God has all the answers to every question and need we will ever have in life. He will teach you how to operate in peace and know His Will.

When we are not convinced of this, we live in doubt and unbelief, which blocks the blessings from God. We can sit in church, worship and raise our hands, but when a crisis occurs, do we run to God or run to the phone? Do you actually believe that God is in control and will turn all things out for your good? These are questions that must be answered before we can please God.

It is impossible to please God without faith. *We must become childlike in our faith and believe God at His every Word!* He is Truth and Life! God can answer prayers even in the midst of what seems to be the darkest days of life. My nephew injured his collar bone during a baseball game and had to go to the hospital. God used the situation to bring family together to reveal a truth to his mother. God is faithful. He turns all things out for our good and His glory.

Paul exhorts us, "My God shall supply all your need according to His riches in glory by Christ Jesus" (Philippians 4:19). The Lord has everything we will ever need stored up for us already. God spent forty years to convince Israel that He was the answer, their full supply, and He was everything they would ever need. They had doubt and unbelief. They murmured and complained. The Bible says:

> The Lord thy God hath blessed thee in all the works of thy hand: he knoweth thy walking through this great wilderness: these forty years the Lord thy God hath been with thee; thou hast lacked nothing.
>
> — DEUTERONOMY 2:7

God was letting them know His arm was not short and He had full supply. Jesus Christ is our Promised Land! When we abide in Him there is never any lack. He is constantly present in us when we have received Him as Savior. When we want Him as Savior but not as Lord, we experience lack due to rebellion and ignorance. God used Moses to lead three million Israelites through the wilderness, so how on earth could you have doubt about Him leading you through? When you choose to get into self-pity, you are telling God you doubt His care and provision.

The quickest way to get through the desert or wilderness is to step over into spiritual growth, trust God, and have a teachable spirit to learn what God is trying to impart into your soul. When we react out of our emotions, we stay in doubt, unbelief, murmuring and complaining, and crazy-making mode, and we live in drama. The Lord showed me this is the **devil racing after my assignment** (drama). The Lord gave me this many years ago. Can you see the enemy's plan? If he can get you stuck in drama, you won't take one step forward in your destiny with God.

To get out of drama, stop talking about the pain and focus on Jesus and His ways! His ways are in His Word! His promises are in His Word! Maybe you find that hard to believe. It doesn't matter where you find yourself right now, God is still faithful, and His arm is not shortened. If you will seek God, He will give you wisdom, knowledge, and grace that will carry you through whatever trial you are facing. He will carry you through as you trust Him fully and wait on Him. Choose to obey God and watch Him bring His blessing into your life. Blessing is on the other side of obedience. His anointing in our life produces restoration, favor, supernatural progress, and change of status. We become authentic when we surrender our old self and old ways of doing things for God's ways. People will begin to notice and say, "This is the Lord's doing, it is marvelous in our eyes" (Psalm 118:23).

CHAPTER 13

KNOWING GOD AS FATHER

He Sees and Cares

God goes out of His way to let us know He sees our location. Your location today may be one of desperation, rejection, hopelessness, anger, or a whole host of other emotions; but God is still on the throne and cares deeply for you. I know in my own personal life, God confirms to me that He sees every situation whether He uses a bumper sticker, a billboard or a scripture that lets me know He is making me aware of His constant care and presence.

Earlier today, we took one of our cars to a tire store to get new tires. Tonight, after dinner, we went to pick it up. After getting in the car, I suddenly realized I did not have my phone, or at least I thought I didn't. I motioned for my husband to call me so I could locate my phone. Needless to say, I drove straight back to the restaurant to look for my phone when Dan pulled up beside me holding my phone up. I had left it in his vehicle on the drive over. This delayed us a few minutes. On our drive home I encountered five deer that had just made it across the road in front of me and were climbing the hill. I realized that had I not thought I had left my phone in the restaurant, I might have been in an accident with the deer. You see, God used our circumstances to produce a delay to protect us from harm.

God seems to go overboard to make me aware of His presence that gives me great assurance of His provision. This is His amazing love. There is no other like Him. He is amazing! His love never fails. He is a great Father.

I remember talking to my mother a few weeks ago about a situation that brought great hurt to our family. We were discussing how everything in this situation had gone to the barn. We drove by a bank where I noticed a vehicle with a bumper sticker, "Gone to the Barn." Talk about God letting us know He sees every single thing is amazing! Sometimes He has a sense of humor, and other times He just wants to remind us of His constant presence. Either way, it is truly amazing. This is the love of Father God!

Since our perception of Father God is based on our experience with our earthly father, we can sometimes have a wrong perception of God. One might think God has a huge baseball bat, ready to take you out at any given moment if you mess up. Others might think they can get away with anything if they grew up with a father that bailed them out of everything and gave them everything they wanted.

I believe God monitors my every move and will at the sweet times let me know He is watching. He wants to encourage me when I feel down or am disappointed. If you know any people, you will experience disappointment.

God sees every tear, every move, and every broken heart! The Bible says:

> Casting all your care upon him; for he careth for you.
> —1 Peter 5:7, kjv

> The eyes of the Lord are upon the righteous, and his ears are open unto their cry...The righteous cry, and the Lord heareth, and delivereth them out of all their troubles.
> —Psalm 34:15, 17, kjv

"Like as a father pitieth his children, so the Lord pitieth them that fear Him" (Psalm 103:13). The Hebrew word for "pity" here means to "fondle, cuddle, love, be compassionate."[1] God wants us to climb up in His lap and allow Him to wrap His arms of love around us while bringing our cares to

Him. He gently touches your cheeks and says, "I love you" when you need it the most.

Many Christians go through life thinking God is angry at them or they have blown it too many times for God to forgive them. They believe they can never please Him. Let's take a look at the life of David, the man after God's own heart (1 Samuel 13: 14). He sinned through adultery, murder, and lying, but repented, and God used him greatly! David was not a perfect man. There is hope for any of us when we actually read the Bible and see the lives of the people God chose to use for His purposes.

God knows our every move and feels our pain. He is moved with compassion toward us. He knows we are frail. God is not mad at you. He has loving, precious thoughts about you. If you feel you have messed up beyond all hope, it is you that God is speaking to today. Cry out to Him as the Israelites did. Each time the Israelites cried out to God, He came and answered their cry. God is waiting for you to run to Him. He loves you and still has a great plan for your life if you will truly repent and turn from a life of sin and secrecy.

WILL GOD REALLY HELP ME?

Many Christians know God is able but struggle with His willingness because they feel unworthy. You are a priceless treasure to Him, even with the dirt you may feel around you in your present situation. You may realize you truly chose a wrong path and went from being a carpenter to chasing chickens at night, and failed miserably at your marriage, or you may have ignored the warnings from God and lost a business deal. Whatever your struggle, God is still waiting to help you!

You may be offended at the people who truly know you and love you, but because of sin in your life that you know they are aware of, you distance yourself from them through self-destruction. You may have gotten offended at someone, even perhaps the pastor or another leader at your church. The enemy is trying to block your blessings from God. When you get offended, you can no longer receive the blessing. Forgive and move on. Forgiving does not cancel consequences, but it assures us of being able to step out of the prison of bitterness. It is for our own good to forgive.

We are to ask God and believe in faith that He will answer our prayers. The Bible says, "Let him ask in faith, nothing wavering. For he that wavereth is like a wave of the sea driven with the wind and tossed. For let not that man think that he shall receive any thing of the Lord" (James 1:6–7).

The Bible tells us that the Israelites murmured and complained, but cried out to God to help them. Each time, God heard their cry and came to help them. Each time they went against God's leader and plan, they continued their journey in the wilderness because God had much to teach them. They wanted to return to bondage. Think about it with me for a minute. Can you imagine being fed fresh manna from heaven from God? Can you see the Red Sea parting and the Israelites walking over on dry land? What do you suppose caused them to doubt?

The Israelites cried out to God from their sin, backslidden condition, and idolatry, and God heard their cry and answered. God is saying the same thing to us today. *"You can call upon Me, you can cry out to Me, and I will hear."* Are you afflicted today? Do you feel you are in bondage in any area of your life? Perhaps you believe God has turned a deaf ear to you because of some detestable or shameful sin. No matter what you are facing and no matter what you have done, God still cares and hears your cries. He wants us to learn to trust Him fully. God will put a wall of fire about you that the enemy is unable to penetrate when you run to Him in sincere repentance. He is waiting to hear from you right now. Turn your heart toward heaven and cry out to God for His help. He is waiting and willing. Do not believe the lies of the enemy any longer. God cares for YOU!

THE BOTTOM

When you feel you are at the bottom of the barrel or flat on your back that is a great place to be. There is no place to look, but up! God is there waiting. For many believers, sinking to the bottom of a situation is an end in itself. They become so overwhelmed with where they find themselves, they think there is no light in sight. They develop a sense of unworthiness due to wrong choices, or perhaps something that happened to them due to ignoring warnings. No matter what the circumstances, we can feel overwhelmed at times, if we choose to allow our emotions to control us.

Over time, believers may begin to feel trapped. Isaiah wrote, "O thou afflicted, tossed with tempest, and not comforted" (Isaiah 54:11). Some believers even get mad at God. They get weary in waiting and begin to flip and flop between walking in the Spirit and allowing their emotions to get the best of them. This is when we must double-up on our Word intake.

Some allow the enemy to convince them that God no longer cares and fall into spiritual apathy. They wake up each morning feeling like their head is in the fog and just can't seem to get out of bed. They drink a latte with caffeine and force themselves through the day. Does this sound like a place you have ever visited?

When we are truly convicted and repent, we are not to stay in the mire of sin and despair. We are forgiven and get up through the victory of the cross of Jesus Christ!

The Lord hears our cry. The Bible tells us, "Do not say, 'I will recompense evil'; Wait for the LORD, and He will save you" (Proverbs 20:22, NKJV). David held onto his faith and God met him. "This poor man cried, and the Lord heard him, and saved him out of all his troubles" (Psalm 34:6). The Lord will do the same for you! He is no respecter of persons.

GOD IS OUR DADDY

Whether you have come from a broken home or had a great childhood with wonderful parents, God is still Daddy, "Abba Father" (Vines). God wants to redeem painful years and memories. If you have a memory that causes pain, you are in need of healing. Isn't it amazing that even the slightest fragrance can bring back a whole host of memories? An old song can bring back a memory of an old relationship. God wants us healthy and desires that we come to know Him as Daddy.

Eating dinner as a family, without the distraction of television or phones, is a vital part of any healthy family life. Dinner is a great time to show a deep interest in your children's lives by asking questions and taking the time to listen from your heart to their answers. This establishes the belief in our children that Daddy and Mommy care about their day and how they feel.

It is also a great time to ask questions of our spouse. Date nights are necessary to establish bonding time as well, especially if there are young children in the home. God is the same. He cares! He wants us to establish a set time with Him as well. Develop the habit of spending time with Him first thing in the morning and talk to Him all throughout the day.

Just as we eat to live, we must feed our spirit with the Word of God to live. We must choose to develop the daily discipline of alone time with God. We must choose to shut out all distractions so we can hear what God is saying to our hearts.

Time spent together is meaningful and strengthens bonds. Playing together, praying together, laughing together, eating together, and attending church together are all healthy habits. Time spent with God is imperative to our growth. Our personal alone time with God is vital to knowing God as Daddy.

When we spend time with family we show we care because we communicate. Talk to your kids every day. Talk to your spouse every day. Talk to God and ask Him for wisdom and direction. God will speak to you through His Word and others. His instructions always line up with His Word, the Bible.

God has a sense of humor and wants us to laugh. There is something wonderful about spending time with your parents and laughing about silly things. Parents and children grow closer together and learn what's important to each other through finding a common interest, playing, and laughing together. Friends also grow closer together spending time together and laughing.

Prayer is essential in our families and with our Father God. Your children and those around you will mimic your actions. Children are like mirrors; they reflect what they see. When we spend time with God, we become more like Him. When you pray with your spouse and children, you are showing them the most important relationship in your life is with God.

Expensive games or the latest technological gizmos could never replace time spent with Daddy. Just as children desperately want what money can't buy—their Daddy's love and attention—God wants us to have that kind of relationship with Him. The focus on accomplishments, on work, or other distractions are not as important to God as our time spent with Him. The same goes with our family. Care enough to leave a lasting legacy of eternity by leading your family to know God as Daddy.

When we walk through our own alone times, our own personal trials and deserts, we will cherish our time spent with God. He is a great God, a great Father, and wants to rescue us. He allows us to walk through things so we can grow and learn to trust Him. What lesson have you missed? We don't ever fail tests with our heavenly Father. We just get to take them over!

CHAPTER 14

THE SECRET TO FULFILLMENT

Look Toward the Heavenly Father

I s the ability to be powerful or in control of everything fulfilling to you? Is the ability to manipulate others fulfilling? Is the ability to identify a hurt and help heal it fulfilling? Is the ability to find a need and help meet it fulfilling? Surrendering your struggle against loneliness involves surrendering to God. You will move faster through to healing when you begin to help others while you are in a struggle. God will bring people across your path where you can sow a seed of kindness, a good deed, or some other act of kindness.

Make a list of the good things in your life and begin to have an *attitude of gratitude* and be thankful. Ask God to show you what He wants you to learn through your desert or wilderness. Find a trusted counselor or someone of the same sex to share your experience with so you can walk through to healing. Looking to our heavenly Father is the secret of fulfillment.

Married or not, I believe the greatest secret lies in coming to know Jesus as Lord, and our heavenly Father as our heavenly Husband. When we begin to trust God's timing and not our own, we learn to rest. When we focus on our relationship with God, He can then bring healing to the areas of need, and a healthy relationship. When you stop looking for love, you'll find it.

Probably the most devastating time to a woman who has been abandoned by her husband is the night time. This is due to the woman's greatest need being that of security and affection. When she has her husband beside her she feels protected. When we look to our spouse for our worth and value, we are setting a trap for ourselves. We must look to God and learn who we are in Christ to be truly fulfilled. No one can pull the rug out from under you when you truly know who you are in Christ.

There will be a season of grief when one walks through abandonment, which is normal, but you will be able to rise again and move forward. A woman can decide to abandon her family as well. Women are walking out on their husbands and children too. Women are pursuing their "own thing" and forgetting their family. Men are being left with raising children now as well. Men also experience the pain of being alone after betrayal.

Having the comfort of your spouse welcoming you at the door fills a certain gap of loneliness. If you have been married a long time and are going through a separation, this will be your alone time. God is there, but your spouse is not. This is when you must run to God as your heavenly Husband.

See the sunrise! Get up to see the sun and meet with the Son of God. While many can't stand the silence of night after the departure of a spouse, others live in fear, constantly looking over their shoulders. Some marriages are just surviving, but with no real connection. I know people who are married but emotionally detached. Have you ever been at lunch or in a relationship with someone who was not emotionally connected? I remember going to lunch on many occasions with a friend of mine. She would never sit at the table for long. She was always up going around the entire restaurant talking to everyone. She found it hard to sit and focus on conversation with the person in her presence. She apparently thought she would miss something.

When any couple has unresolved hurts, there can be times of emotional detachment where you feel alone even while married. We must look to God to fill that hunger for connection. The emotional wounds are far greater to heal than physical ones. Sometimes, a woman just needs to hear her husband say, "I am sorry" and help her walk through to the place of healing. When a husband says, "Just get over it," he is making her feel worthless.

You may have had to divorce due to abuse or alcohol. Even though things are bad, you will still have a feeling of loneliness because you were used to your spouse being there. No matter what reason a relationship may have ended, there will be times of loneliness.

You may be married and still feel lonely. Whether we find ourselves longing for a husband or a wife, or just long to be emotionally connected to the one we already have, we must learn that we can *know* true fulfillment in the midst of our alone times with God Himself. God is our true source of fulfillment.

WHITE PICKET FENCES

Whether you are a woman or a man reading this, you need to know that most little girls grew up hearing about white picket fences, two dogs, kids, and a home with a husband for life. We all heard about falling in love and living happily ever after. It seems we were fed a fairy tale. You can be married to a man who has a cell phone on his ear, or a business man who travels constantly, where you may find yourself alone. If your spouse seldom communicates, you don't experience the emotional connection that can also make you feel alone as well. Whether single, married, widowed, or divorced, we can all feel alone. Men and women can both feel alone. There are seasons in life, in marriage, and in all relationships. Since God created us for relationship, we can sometimes feel incomplete when we don't have friends or family nearby.

When we walk through the pain of divorce, our white picket fence dream becomes shattered. We can live with shattered dreams. I thank God for my husband now and how he desires to take care of and protect me. Yesterday, he made me feel like a princess as he was simply making sure the car that I primarily drive had safe tires. He is always making sure I am protected. He told me he can buy a new car but he can't replace me as his wife. When you truly become one with your mate, no matter what you are walking through together, life is great in God! I thank God He showed me I can live the dream, even after all I have experienced, because God walked with me and is still with me.

HELP

Since the Garden of Eden, God intended for the woman to be a helper. God said, "It is not good for that man should be alone; I will make him a helper comparable to him" (Genesis 2:18, NKJV). God created women to be partners, helpers, encouragers, companions, lovers, and friends; so at times, if there is no one in our life that we can help, we (women) can get frustrated. There are several categories where we can find ourselves. One is when no one seems to need our help. Second, when someone we truly love no longer *wants* our help; third, when our children grow up and think they no longer *need* our help; fourth, when we find we are *no longer* a help; and lastly, when we become so overwhelmed with people and drama, we feel we *can't* help due to sheer exhaustion. These can make us wonder what on earth we are to do since we were created to help.

God also created women and men in His image (Genesis 1:27). God is love so we were created to love and be loved. Only God can love completely. I know that God created us on purpose, with purpose, with a void that *only He can fill*. Perhaps, as the Samaritan woman found herself at the well at noonday, we too have a deep well inside us that only Jesus, the Living Water, can fill (John 4:14).

We know from the Bible that God is a jealous God (Exodus 20:4–5) and He will have no other gods before Him. He will have no other person before Him. God is the only one who can fill the void. I have found that there is no one but God who can truly be first in my life. To instill hope for the success of marriage, always choose a spouse that puts God first in their life. There is no career or position a man or woman can hold that will fill the void in their life. The void was created by God, and only God can fill it.

I remember speaking at a women's conference and sharing about Jesus being the love of my life. I also remember telling the ladies that we have to stay in agreement with God for our life, our husband, and so on. I gave an example of angels ascending and descending on a ladder from heaven. As we stay in agreement with God, praying His Word over those in our lives, the angels are dispatched from heaven to bring the answer (Psalm 103:20). The enemy tries to get us to murmur and complain so we step into doubt and unbelief. Then the angels are stopped when we get out of agreement. There was one young lady there who was going through a tough time in her marriage. After the meeting, she came up and shared with me that she wanted to work on her marriage. I learned many years later from my nephew that her son was thankful for his mom coming to that meeting. God empowered her to go back to her husband and pray for her marriage. God totally restored them, and they are still married today many years later.

If you are married, begin to pray Malachi 2:6 over your spouse. (No lying can be found in his/her lips. No unrighteousness can be found in them. They walk in peace and integrity with God and turn many others away from iniquity.) One Word from God can change your entire circumstances. That couple is still together today and has a good marriage. Praise God for His resurrection power!

CHAPTER 15

PRICELESS TREASURE

He Will Reveal What He Placed Within You

You are a priceless treasure to God. Now go with me in your mind to your childhood and reflect on times with family. I remember growing up going to the beach on vacation. We would spend endless hours on the beach with our parents helping us make castles in the sand. They were so beautiful, and the time we spent together is worth far more than rubies and gold. Memories and time spent with our parents are priceless. You have to be on the beach or in a sandbox to make a sand castle. Storms in life can position you in the desert with no water in sight. Sometimes we can feel like we are all boxed in with no place to go! It is in these times that we must dig deeper in the Word of God to find His Word for us in this season. Sometimes, He will just speak a *word* to our heart that is exactly what we need.

Instead of allowing whatever storm that put you in the desert defeat, discourage, and destroy you, ask God what He wants you to learn through this time in your life. *We never have a testimony without a test.* The places we walk through equip us to help others. God desires to mold us into a priceless treasure in His hand. God tells us in His Word, "Yet I am always with you; you hold me by my right hand" (Psalm 73:23, NIV). He never lets go of your hand. Even when we want to let go, God holds us even tighter.

Ask God what character flaw He is removing from your life and what lesson you need to learn. Don't blame others, but look at yourself, even in the most painful places. Even if you did not personally cause the storm, ask God what He is speaking to you. Perhaps your husband tells you that you talk too much. Take that to God! Maybe, just maybe, God is telling you to spend more time listening, not only to Him, but to your husband as well. Listen to what your mate is saying.

When the woman was caught in the act of adultery in the Bible, scholars speculate that Jesus was writing the names of her accusers in the sand. Perhaps He was naming specific sins as well, because every accuser dropped their stone and left. Jesus chose to write their sins in the sand, so they too, could be washed away. Jesus did not write them on tablets of stone. God desires to cleanse our accusers as well.

People can be used by the enemy. We have all been used by the enemy unaware. *Don't take your anger and frustration out on others, take it to God and pour out your heart to Him.* You might even want to write a letter to God sharing your heart, then tear it up and throw it away.

Choose to surrender to God in the desert so He can make a castle for you in the sand, so He can make a priceless treasure out of you. He will reveal the hidden treasures He has placed in you as well. I did not know that I was a writer until the Lord revealed it to me. I wake up in the morning hearing Him speaking to me. I see books that He has called me to write. He spoke a scripture to my heart that said, "Write all the words I have spoken to you," and then I had to obey the instruction. That is a hidden treasure that He placed in me. Until I surrendered to His plan, it seemed I lived in defeat without purpose.

We must all choose to surrender to God's deliverance in the desert. Cooperate with God's change in your life, and all of a sudden, you will notice your heart beginning to soften, and you will find that something has changed. Admit you have needs. You must admit you need people in your life to go through God's character development plan. As He develops you, hidden treasures will be revealed to you as well.

The Israelites found themselves at the Red Sea with a sandstorm behind that the enemy created, and it appeared they had come to a dead end. The enemy will create storms to keep you off focus. He will try to make you feel hopeless. I am sure the Israelites felt hopeless and afraid. (See Exodus 14:13–14.) With the Red Sea in front and the sandstorm raging just behind them, they had no place to go. God brought deliverance to them by holding back the Red Sea and allowing them to walk over on dry land. The same Red Sea that God held back to allow the Israelites to cross over was the same Red Sea that God used to destroy their enemies.

God drew a line in the sand for the Israelites. They had a choice to make. They either had to surrender and cooperate with God or be destroyed by the enemy. It is when we choose to die to self and cooperate with God in His character development plan in our life that we find total dependence and trust in God. Even when there seems to be no end in sight, God is holding our right hand.

CHOOSE LOVE

"Love...is not touchy or fretful or resentful; it takes no account of the evil done to it [it pays no attention to a suffered wrong]" (1 Corinthians 13:4–5, AMP). Choosing to respond in love is good for your health. Did you know that? It is proven by medical science that hostility produces stress, which produces tension headaches, ulcers, and all sorts of disease. It creates *dis-ease*.

The little things like the server not giving you unsweetened tea, to the drycleaners messing up your favorite outfit, to the phone call you answered while you were drying your hair, are the small stressors that produce hostility when we don't choose love. Perhaps it is the stoplights that always seem to be red when you show up. It's when your spouse has moved a file or stack of papers that you need at the last minute. Does this sound like something that has ever happened to you?

Your body is filled with rage when you choose to stay bound by hostility and anger. You have to choose love daily. Remember when Jesus called Lazarus forth from the grave? He was alive but was still bound by grave clothing. Jesus told His disciples to loose his grave clothing so he could be free.

Some people are saved but are still walking around in grave clothing. From carrying an old hurt, to staying stuck in the desert, it produces bondage. Jesus came that we might have life and be free. Speak out loud, *"In the Name of Jesus, loose me and let me go! I choose love and put aside hostility, anger, unforgiveness, and selfishness. I choose God's ways. I choose to love!"*

It is a choice and a decision that everyone must make to be free. Surrender to God's ways! (See Proverbs 4:10–27.) To get to a castle in the natural, you have to swim the mote or cross over by the bridge; but either way, you have to cross over. You have to choose to get into the water of God's Word. We come to the Father through His Son Jesus who bridged the gap between us and God the Father, and we learn to live by God's plan. We have to choose to cross over.

CHAPTER 16

A BROKEN HEART

Healed and Made Whole

When we find ourselves in the desert after a storm of abandonment, adultery, betrayal, abuse of any kind, separation, and divorce, we often find ourselves feeling all alone and experience a broken heart. It feels like someone has ripped your heart out of your chest, trampled all over it, and kicked it to the side of the road.

When someone steps out of the covenant of marriage, people don't oftentimes realize how many other lives they are affecting. They are only led by their own selfish desires, which we know come from Satan. He has been doing the same old things for thousands of years, and he knows us better than we know ourselves. He knows our weakness and knows exactly how to try to lead us off the path of righteousness.

Satan comes to steal, kill, and destroy. I remember from my own experiences of abandonment, marital abuse, and betrayal just how great the pain can be. There is no way you can understand unless you have walked in those shoes. You can say what you want, but there is nothing more painful than betrayal through separation and divorce. Death of a spouse is final, but divorce leaves a scar of rejection that only God can heal. No other man or woman can bring healing to those places.

Child abuse produces a life full of fear, rejection, shame, and insecurity. Any injustice or betrayal can break your heart and leave you in extreme pain. Pain draws the heart of God. God is close to the brokenhearted. We must choose to forgive, and ask God to forgive our offender for they do not know what they are doing. Jesus prayed this prayer on the cross. When we choose to live in forgiveness, God opens our eyes to see others the way He sees them, a lost soul.

When we arrive at the place to see people through God's eyes and understand that our spouse or offender is weak and blinded by the enemy, then we can move on with a teachable spirit. Our heart becomes softened, and we grow stronger in our walk with God.

There are times when your emotions feel like a roller coaster and other times when you feel like you are going to make it. At some point, you will begin to feel sorry for your spouse or the people who betrayed or violated you. You will realize that forgiveness does not do away with consequences to bad choices, and learn to take care of yourself emotionally. There is no relationship worth damaging your own soul and health.

God wants us to be able to have His heart and move forward through forgiveness, which releases us from a prison of bitterness. Forgiveness does not mean you condone the sin, but you will get to the place where you realize your mate or offender is apparently a lost soul.

Fleshly lust is a snare that the enemy uses to draw people away that are not totally surrendered to God. All you can do for them is pray for God to save them, open their eyes of understanding, and move forward in your own healing and for your children, if you have any.

The enemy sets you up to continue feeling rejection. You can feel lonely, have a broken heart, but the world still goes on because you can rest in the fact that *He is with you, the Savior of the world.* How consoling it is to know that God knows us, loves us, and does not leave us from the womb to the tomb. God has a great plan in store for your life when you surrender, trust, and obey Him; even in walking through the storms of life that leave you feeling stranded in the desert of pain and loneliness. God is close to the brokenhearted. He turns everything out for our good and His glory. God gives us strength as we turn to Him and He empowers us to walk out each new day.

As you allow your heart to be healed and made whole, you will see the negative cycles broken, such as short-lived relationships, debt, marriage, and family problems. You will have a passion for life and purpose! You will begin to have fun in your relationships, enjoy your area of work more, and you will recognize a divine sense of destiny. So, how is your heart? Your heart determines the quality of your life!

CHAPTER 17

HOLY BOLDNESS AFTER THE DESERT

Renewed Strength

When you have a healed heart, God will empower you to help bring healing to others. Ask Him for boldness. "Now when they saw the boldness of Peter and John, and perceived that they were unlearned and ignorant men, they marveled; and they took knowledge of them, that they had been with Jesus" (Acts 4:13).

People will begin to see the change in you as you spend time with Jesus. He changes us on the inside, and it shows on the outside by the way we respond to others and our heart attitude. God will give you renewed strength and boldness as you seek Him with your whole heart in the midst of the desert.

Just as Peter and John stood waiting for judgment to be pronounced, the man who had just received healing stood with them. The synagogue rulers looked on, "beholding the man which was healed standing with them, they could say nothing against it" (Acts 4:14). People will notice you are healed and have made it through the desert when you come forth as a priceless treasure in the hand of God, fit for His use, with a heart like His and ready to help others who find themselves in the places you have walked. God will equip you to help others build sand castles in the desert rather than staying lost in the sand.

It is pretty obvious that Peter and John had to have seen the look on the high priest's face when they knew they had been with Jesus. The saints in Jerusalem rejoiced with the two disciples. Then they prayed, "Lord, behold their threatenings: and grant unto thy servants, that with all boldness they may speak they word, by stretching forth thine hand to heal; and that signs and wonders may be done by the name of thy holy child Jesus" (Acts 4:29–30). The saints were thanking God for the boldness He had given the disciples. They began to thank God and realized it was only the beginning. They, too, prayed to speak with boldness and holy assurance, and for God to provide visible evidence that He was with them. God is with us today.

AFTER THE STORM OF DIVORCE

After the marriage has ended and you have come to a place of healing, you come to a place of realization that God is your husband. What will our marriage with the Lord be like? I have often taught that our marriage here on earth is a training ground for preparation for heaven and gives us a glimpse of what a marriage with Christ will be like. A marriage with Christ will be a perfect union of unconditional love and trust. It will be one of complete transparency, sensitivity, security, provision, tenderness, and complete fulfillment. Our marriage in heaven will be perfect. You will be treated as a priceless treasure, His most sought-after beautiful bride.

When God see us, we are His. If you begin to think of a husband-and-wife relationship here on earth in comparison, you won't have a proper picture of marriage to God, because it is not a sexual relationship. We think of God in the proper biblical role and responsibility a husband holds. A husband befriends his wife, comforts, encourages, protects, provides, and loves her. God does all this far more perfectly than any man is capable.

You don't ignore your husband or think less of him when I speak of the Lord being your husband. You and I are taught to pray, respect, honor, help, and love our husbands. You must not set unrealistic expectations of your husband as this adds stress to him because he will never measure up to God.

We love our earthly husbands and submit to their leadership as we trust God and seek Him with our whole heart.

How your relationship is with your husband, right now, might give you a glimpse of how your relationship stands with the Lord. The same goes for men with their wives. Are you angry, distrusting, or expecting more than he can give at times? God is the ultimate giver, and we must realize our husbands are human.

We must realize that only God is able to meet all of our emotional needs. God uses our mate to bring healing to us when we love God and put Him first. We usually marry people with opposite strengths and weaknesses. This helps us learn balance. We find we have need of each other. Jeremiah 17:5–6 tells us that when we depend on people or our mate for fulfillment, we will stay in the wilderness. God never intended for our mate to fill the void in our life that can only be filled by God. We are not to place our husband or wife above God in our life. God tells us in His Word He is a jealous God. God must come first. Men and women alike cannot expect to have all their needs met through their spouse. It is only God who can fill the void.

CHAPTER 18

SECRET TO SUCCESS

An Eternal Imprint of God's Word

Our secret to success is found in the Lion of the Tribe of Judah and the Word of God. Last night we were at dinner in a local restaurant where two meetings were being held. One was the local Lion's Club, and the other was a Water Club. I could overhear the conversation about the intake of healthy water for our life. This is so true, not only for our physical life but also for our spiritual life. We are children of the Most High King. He is the Lion of the Tribe of Judah! We have the water of God's Word to keep us as we apply it to our lives and circumstances.

The enemy imitates a lion by roaring to scare us to stop us from moving. Repent from any murmuring and complaining, ask God to give you a pure heart so you can hear and see, keep your eyes on Jesus, the Word of God, and keep moving forward. God is saying to each of us: Beloved, separate yourself from everything that instills fear and brings confusion. Refuse to allow anything to undermine your peace and stability in God. If you will do this, you will be able to see clearly the attack of the enemy against you, which will then position you to resist him while you maintain spiritual integrity. God will give you this insight when you set your mind and heart on Him.

"Be sober, be vigilant; because your adversary the devil walks about like a roaring lion, seeking whom he may devour. Resist him, steadfast in the faith, knowing that the same sufferings are experienced by your brotherhood in the world" (1 Peter 5:8–9). God never ceases to amaze me how He gives us natural manifestations of what is happening in the spirit. We are constantly surrounded by Him, the Lion of the Tribe of Judah, and His Word when we seek Him and correspond with action by speaking His Word in agreement. When we magnify the Word of God in our lives, it brings with it the favor of God and man. Favor is an unexplained disposition and unexpected investment in your well-being by others. When the Word of God is magnified, your love walk opens the door of empowerment to success. Your love walk is directly linked to the power of the Holy Spirit in your life. The Bible says, "My son, do not forget my teaching, but keep my commands in your heart, for they will prolong your life many years and bring you prosperity. Let love and faithfulness never leave you; bind them around your neck, write them on the tablet of your heart. Then you will win favor and a good name in the sight of God and man" (Proverbs 3:1–4, NIV). I strongly recommend you study and pray Proverbs 3 every day. Jesus told us in Scripture: "Love the Lord your God with all your heart and with all your soul and with all your mind" (Matthew 22:37, NIV).

RETURN TO YOUR FIRST LOVE

Is Jesus your first love? Is He the one you think of first thing in the morning? Do you wake up excited to speak to Him? Does your heart linger at the thought of seeing Him face to face one day? Do you wake up sometimes and hear yourself speaking to the Lord from your heart? This is a picture of a perfect engagement.

I remember when I came through to the other side of healing after abandonment, abuse, betrayal, cancer, divorce, and damaged emotions. I came to know the Lord on a totally new level. He walked with me, and He talked with me and made me feel like a favorite child. He let me know that I was special to Him and that He created me for a special purpose.

He wants to have that same relationship with all his children. We, as Christians, and the church who is the body of Christ, are being prepared as His beautiful bride, without spot and blemish. Do you and I long for the day when we will be joined to our Love and Lord Jesus Christ forever? We should all have that kind of deep abiding longing in our hearts. When we choose to make our relationship with Him a priority, we will know true fulfillment, even in the darkest places when we walk through the desert.

Our corresponding actions with our Lover and Lord are to communicate with God about everything. We need to tell him all the little things that build up over time and aggravate us so that we won't become agitated in our spirit man. Tell God about the little things and the big things. Tell Him your secret desires. Tell God when you feel angry, hurt, aggravated, disappointed, excited, overwhelmed, and amazed by His love, and you will find that you have less to complain about to your husband or wife and friends. The more time you spend with God, the more your husband or wife will be drawn to you, for they will be unable to resist Jesus in you.

If you are not married, tell God about the details of your day, tell Him about your desires for a mate or whatever your dream may be in life. He truly cares about the details. He is the best friend you will ever have, and since He sees and knows everything anyway, why not pour out your heart to Him?

Secondly, you must choose to trust God in the great days and in the desert places, or the darkest times in which you find yourself. God desires that you know Him and trust Him above all else. He is the One who will provide for you, protect you, and instruct you in ways to go, just as you would look to a husband for his input.

If you are a man reading this, tell God the same. Tell Him your every desire. Tell Him about your day at work. Begin to read the book of Proverbs for His wisdom. Start reading the Bible through with a plan. There are many Bibles available that have reading plans already in them.

Trust is a key element in every relationship. When we are hurt, we need that freedom to express our feelings without a sense of abandonment or fear of loss and rejection. Look to God's Word for direction for everything in life.

The Bible tells us that God owns all the cattle and all the hills. (See Psalm 50:10.) I tell God sometimes that if He has to sell a couple cows, I am sure He won't mind at all. Now we all know God does not have to sell a cow to meet my needs. He can move on a Texan with a ranch full of cows to sell them and bless someone. God has a sense of humor. God is all-knowing, as I have stated before, so He will never leave us nor forsake us. He never makes a mistake. Knowing this gives you a sense of peace that passes all understanding once you step over into faith in God.

Instead of putting all your demands and expectations on your mate, start asking God for His help and input. If you are single, this will help you to keep in mind that God is all powerful, all knowing, and created the universe. He can handle anything.

Third, remember you are a co-laborer with God in life. Share your time, finances, concerns, devotion and adoration, plans, love, and loyalty; and you can lay down the fear or worry of God taking you for granted. He knows the very number of hairs on your head. He is so amazing. Our life with God is a daily partnership. We commit our day to Him, surrender our life to Him, and He comes alongside to comfort, help, teach, keep, protect, instruct, and love us all the days of our lives. What an amazing partnership. (See 2 Corinthians 6:1.)

When we get our hearts broken at a young age in relationships, I like to refer to the problem as our "picker" is broken. We don't see clearly and are sometimes naïve. We can go from one relationship to the next, in and out of marriages looking for fulfillment, and realize we are more alone at heart than ever before. You can also begin to feel unworthy. It is a sense of emptiness and barrenness of the soul. The day God opened my eyes to my First Love was the day I realized I did not need a man to bring fulfillment, He was all I needed, this man Jesus!

BEYOND THE VEIL

I came face to face with Him as He touched me at a church service one night where an evangelist from Australia was ministering. I'll never forget it! He asked the audience that whoever wanted a closer relationship with the Lord to come forward for prayer. I went forward immediately and stood for prayer. I remember being slain in the Holy Spirit and lying on the floor. I felt something brush over my face, and I saw the Lord kneel down and ever so softly kiss my cheek like my daddy always has. Then He whispered to me, "I love you." I knew I had seen the Lord and felt His touch. Then He removed the veil from my eyes, allowing me to see into the throne room of God, seeing angels standing all around with no space between them. He opened my eyes to see *beyond the veil* into the spirit realm. I remember the sense of awesome awareness and the glory that filled my life that night. No one, and I mean no one, can ever take that away from me.

After coming back to be seated, I asked a friend next to me who did not go up for prayer if the church ladies were placing any scarves or coverings over the ladies' legs as they do in some services. He told me no. I was reflecting on what I felt gently brush across my face. I thought it was probably a prayer cloth, but it was not. It was the Lord Himself.

The evangelist mentioned a book called *Visions Beyond the Veil* for deeper reading, so I ran out the next day in search of it.[1] As I began to read the book, there was a chapter on this group of nine-year-olds who had such radical childlike faith that God removed the veil from their eyes, allowing them to see into the throne room of God. They expressed in the book how there was no space between the angels standing round about God's throne.

At that moment, again, I knew that God had removed the veil from my eyes and given me a glimpse of heaven. God used the book to confirm what He had allowed me to experience. Oh, He is so amazing. The Lover of my Soul, this man Jesus! He delights in me and tells me I am His. He sings over me and longs for relationship with me. I have never felt alone again. The Lord made such an eternal imprint in my life that I would never be the same again.

CHAPTER 19

WHEN LIFE DOES NOT
TURN OUT AS PLANNED

You Are Not Alone

God promises us as women that He will be our heavenly Husband. He promises to fill our heart with Himself. That is exactly what God has done for me. He will do that for you as well. God's promises are true for men and women alike. He is no respecter of persons. God also promises in Psalm 68:5 that He is "a father of the fatherless, a judge for the widows," and "God makes a home for the lonely" (Psalm 68:5–6, NASB).

It is His presence that makes us aware of His all encompassing love, protection, and provision. If you want to live a life filled with love and peace, ask God to become everything to you and fill the void in your life as well. Begin to spend your life in the Word every available moment. Listen to the Word in your car, read the Word, think on the Word, and you will be filled with the Word! You can listen to the Word of God even while you are sleeping at night. The Word of God in you activates the promises of God in your life. You will begin to see change. Expect great things from God!

Whether you are a man or a woman reading this now, God is our heavenly Father and delights in us. God promises to take care of us, and He desires that we trust Him above all else. Pray and believe the Word of God.

For example, "And they said, Believe on the Lord Jesus Christ, and thou shalt be saved, and thy house" (Acts 16:31, KJV). We know *saved* means— eternal life—healed, delivered, set free, nothing missing, nothing broken!

Let's take a look at circumstances the enemy uses to hinder your growth in God. Take a look at the various ways the enemy tries to cripple you and stop your destiny. Learn to rise above your circumstances through magnifying God and His Word. Whatever you magnify becomes greater.

ABANDONED, SINGLE AGAIN, ALONE AS A PARENT

When life does not turn out as planned, it is then that we can really feel the pain of being alone in the desert. A very dear person to me was married for twenty-one years and had dated this man for nine years. When he walked out on her she felt as her whole life had fallen apart. She found herself in the throws of all the financial responsibility, managing the home, the kids, and was emotionally devastated with the abandonment herself. She also had to take a leave of absence from work due to the stress from betrayal. She experienced rejection, loss, anger, rage, and times of crying that most would consider a breakdown; but God, through all this, allowed her to have a breakthrough.

It is when we come to a place where we are abandoned, broken, desperate, sad, angry, rejected, and emotionally distraught that we meet the man of our dreams. His name is Jesus! He comes to pick up the pieces and surround you with His love through family and friends to help you walk again.

The same thing can happen to a man, so I am not singling out just women. Despite the times she felt all alone in the world to the times of peace, she finally found she could laugh again. As a matter of fact, she told me she thought it was the first time she had laughed in a long time.

After lying beside the same man for twenty-one years, a woman can feel extreme pain and loneliness. The loss of security is far greater for a woman than a man. Then there are the children. Oh my! She has to take care of the children through the fallout of the sin that left them in a desert as well. They have emotions and feelings too. Most people don't realize that sin damages the entire family and has a rippling effect like a stone thrown in a lake or stream.

She has to become both Mom and Dad for a season. The role of parenting was never intended to be done alone. Children need their parents, a mother and a father. You have to turn to God for His direction, learn to depend on Him and ask for help. God goes out of His way to make us know He sees every single thing.

God blesses us when we walk through seasons of pain silently and secretly. He rewards us openly for what He sees us do in secret. It is during the midnight hours of crying out to God one minute, reading scriptures the next, to reading a book on damaged emotions, that God makes Himself known. We must choose to encourage ourselves in the Lord and in His Word.

Sometimes the stress of thinking about having to keep up with the home maintenance, a full-time job, and paying the bills is overwhelming. This is when family stands by and surrounds each other to help walk with them through this season of transition. And I do mean transition.

I remember one Sunday God changed the entire order of the church service to let a dear friend know He saw the pain of her broken relationship. That is the amazing love of God. I remember God doing this for me years ago. I was walking through my own season of difficulty and extreme pain. God had given me a song that I had written down on paper earlier in the week. I felt rejected and abandoned but heard the Lord speak to me to go to a particular service at a local ministry. Some friends were going with me and decided to cancel at the last minute, but I went alone anyway. The worship leader began to sing and play the piano and shared how the Lord spoke to his heart that there was a young woman who was going through an extremely painful season in life and God wanted her to know how much He loved her. I remember him saying, just like it was yesterday, "And God says to tell you He gave you a song you wrote on paper this week so you will know it is you." Wow! Can you imagine how special I felt to God? The God of the universe interrupted the service just to let me know He saw the pain in my heart and to let me know how much He loved me. The worship leader heard from God and obeyed by speaking what He heard from God Himself.

I remember going forward to worship and the remaining congregation followed as well. The entire order of the service was changed to a night of worship. What an amazing picture of God's love and mercy! Are you beginning to see the amazing love of God available to you?

Do you remember Hagar in the Bible? She is another example of God's amazing love and protection. God had promised Abraham and Sarah a child and that from that child there would be an entire nation. Years passed to the point where they began to doubt God's promise to them. Sarah decided to take matters into her own hands and told Abraham he could take Hagar, her Egyptian maid, in hopes to bear this promised son. Naturally, when Hagar was with child, Sarah became jealous, mistreated her and sent her away into the desert. *Does this sound familiar?*

While Hagar was in her own desert she met God. He told her He saw and instructed her to go back home to Abraham and Sarah to bear the child. God let her know He had a plan for this child. In response (there is the corresponding action again) to God's Word to Hagar, she called the place "El Roi," meaning, "the God who sees."

Hagar met God in the desert and came to know Him. This is the place where you and I also come to really know God. When things are going wonderful or we are in a place of abundance, we easily get distracted with the cares of the world and have a human tendency to think we don't need God. Oh, how wrong!

God gave Hagar strength to go back home and give birth to the child. When Hagar realized that the God of the universe knew and understood, she had faith to believe for anything. She believed God at His every Word. Do you?

Someone very dear to my heart experienced abandonment in her marriage recently and found herself at the same place she was at six years before when she learned her husband was having an affair with a relative. She forgave and took him back thinking everything was going to be okay. They went through counseling, but he never took the time to develop trust with his wife again. Then it all came out again. Same thing, same relative, same betrayal again! They had been married over twenty years.

Can you imagine the pain and heartache? What devastation again! You might be experiencing a similar situation now. Don't give up. Twelve years later, Hagar experienced pain at the hand of Sarah again. When Sarah finally had her promised son from God, she shouted to Abraham one day, "Get rid of that slave woman and her son" as she was worried about the promise given to Abraham from God, "for that slave woman's son will never share in the inheritance with my son Isaac" (Genesis 21:10).

Can you imagine how Hagar must have felt again? Don't you think she must have been overwhelmed, at least for a moment? Her natural mind must have thought, "Here we go again."

Hagar left again, taking only water and food from Abraham. After awhile, the provisions ran out and she placed Ishmael under a shaded bush in the desert telling the Lord she could not bear to watch her son die. She fell on the ground sobbing before the Lord about her situation she found herself in again! Have you ever fallen to the ground in utter desperation and sobbed your heart out to the Lord? Your husband may have walked out on you and you found yourself holding onto his leg with the children on the ground begging their father not to leave. Sir, your wife may have abandoned you and the children. Your father may have always told you that you would never amount to anything! It is in these times we must remember God is "the God who sees" and never leaves us or forsakes us.

After the angel of God called out to her, he asked her what was the matter, told her not to be afraid, and said that God had heard the cries. He gave her an instruction: "Lift the boy up and take him by the hand, for I will make him into a great nation" (Genesis 21:18). God opened Hagar's eyes, and she saw a well of water. There is the well again. Remember earlier, the Samaritan woman? Hagar filled her vessel with water and gave her son water as well. Hagar and Ishmael came through the desert. God was with them. The Bible tells us, "God was with the boy as he grew up. He lived in the desert and became an archer" (Genesis 21:20, NIV). Hagar filled herself with the water and gave her son water as well. On a spiritual note, when we find the Living Water, Jesus, and begin to fill ourselves with the Word of God, we, too, will make it through the desert. *God is calling out to you today!*

CHAPTER 20

GOD KNOWS YOUR NAME

He Is Interested in the Details

G od calls out to us and knows us by name. I remember after I made it through the desert, the Lord spoke to my heart to change my name to Deborah. I asked the Lord if I was hearing Him clearly. I got in my car and the next message on the tape player (at the time) was a message about how God changed Abram and Sarai's names. He added the "ah" which is the breath of God. I asked God for a second confirmation. As I was driving home, I stopped by the mailbox to get my mail. I had a piece of mail with *Deborah* on it instead of Debbie. I obeyed God and went through the legal process of changing my name. I asked my parents and told them what God had instructed. Isn't it amazing that my parents named me Debbie to start with, as I have found most are named Deborah and go by the nickname Debbie? God knew He was going to change my name before I was ever born. My name legally changed that year on February 14th, Valentine's Day. God has a way of doing things that make you very aware of His love and His plan, step by step.

God has a great plan for you and me, no matter where we find ourselves today. Just as Hagar found herself in the desert and full of hopelessness, God called her by name. God called me by name, and He is still calling out today. God is still calling out today to women with broken hearts who find themselves in the desert. He is also calling out to men who have found themselves in a broken and barren place, whether it was due to some other person's sin or something you did wrong yourself. He deeply cares for you and me.

God has ways of letting each of us know He is actively involved in our lives and sees the details. I remember one beautiful Saturday afternoon after leaving the church I thought I saw a dear friend of mine's son driving a BMW. I knew he was coming to the area to visit his mom and just thought that was the type car he drove. When he came to our connect class that morning, I mentioned to him how I thought I saw him in a BMW. He told me it wasn't him. I remember telling him, "Maybe that is a prophetic word and God is just showing me the type car you will have next."

After class in the sanctuary, he shared with me that he had been looking at BMWs. He said he had written down on paper BMW/Lexus as that was his desire for his next car purchase. He also shared that the night before he searched the newspaper for BMWs. This was God's way of showing him in a very special way that God saw his heart, saw his desire for a particular type car, and that God sees the details. God will use things in the natural to get our attention and make His presence known so that we trust Him in the big things.

It is not about what type car you drive, but God will use natural circumstances to make His presence known in our lives so that we learn to trust Him. He is amazing that way. God uses people to confirm and connect the dots on the pages of our lives, when we allow Him and step out in obedience.

A couple weeks later, the Lord spoke to my heart to email this same man that had visited our class and ask him if he had purchased a black BMW. I stopped and did what I sensed the Lord speaking to me. The next morning, I received a response sharing that at the time he received my email he was driving from Virginia to Winston-Salem, and before 5:00 p.m. that evening he was driving his new black BMW. You see, God made Himself known to this young man in a very personal way. My husband and I had watched this young man as he honored his precious mother while she walked through cancer for an entire year. God was blessing this man with a desire of his heart in the natural. That is the love of God. He certainly knows exactly how to get our attention. He lets us know He knows our name and is interested in the details of our lives.

CHAPTER 21

GOD KNOWS AND UNDERSTANDS YOUR FEARS

Don't Believe the Lies of the Enemy

God told Hagar not to be afraid. I have noticed that when an angel of the Lord shows up or God tells one of His servants not to be afraid, there is a struggle ahead. He warns us that fear will come, but not to be afraid as we face our fears. In most cases, what we think is a big deal is not so hard to get through if we just face the issues one day at a time. It is when we try to figure it all out and control the situation that we have the propensity to operate in fear. I think God brings light to circumstances or painful issues that we need to finally deal with. Other times, it might be a cheating spouse that God exposes so they find opportunity for salvation. God knows the fear of providing for a household after the loss of a husband to death or abandonment. Gently still, we hear, "Do not be afraid, God has heard..." and then God offers advice to Hagar by telling her to lift up the boy.

Hagar probably remembered the harsh words from Sarah and had to choose to believe the Lord or the negative word she had heard from Sarah. Because Hagar trusted in the Lord, she believed God rather than the words that she heard from Sarah. Have you ever had anyone tell you that you would never amount to anything? Perhaps someone told you that you could not make a marriage work. What about this one, "You think God can use you?" or the devil reminding you of your past failures. None of these moved Hagar because she had learned to trust in God. God told Hagar He would make Ishmael into a great nation too. God had a plan for Ishmael.

No matter what you have experienced, God still has a great plan for you and your children too. Don't believe the lies of the enemy.

CHAPTER 22

SEEING GOD'S PROVISION

Trust God, Not People

Moving from the land of *derision* to seeing God's *provision* happens in the desert. Have you ever been ridiculed or made fun of because of something you did or something that happened to you? Have you ever found yourself in the middle of chaos that caused you great pain? I can only imagine that Hagar must have felt shame, disgrace, abandonment, and rejection.

However, God opened Hagar's eyes so she could see clearly. He allowed her to see the well of water (Genesis 21:19) in the desert. God could have performed a miracle and suddenly put a well in the desert. However, the scripture tells us that God opened her eyes. Perhaps she saw something that was there all along, but just hadn't noticed yet because of her pain. Have you ever been walking with a friend and you could see something they could not see? We can get blinded in pain and find sand in our eyes in the desert of derision, which prevents us from seeing God's provision.

When we listen to the contemptuous remarks from people who are being used by the enemy, we find ourselves in the desert of derision and sometimes are unable to see God's provision that is right in front of us. Once God opens our eyes, we move from derision to provision. You can feel so ridiculed by people and circumstances that you have blind spots and are unable to see what is right in front of you. The enemy tries to keep you from moving forward and seeing God's plan of victory.

Maybe you find yourself in the land of derision right down where things really look hopeless. Perhaps you don't have the natural strength to move forward due to all the stress from your current situation. Maybe you are contemplating all the months ahead and wondering how on earth you are going to make it. Do you find yourself in this same desert wondering how you are going to provide for your children, make the house payments, go to work and function with excellence, or just get out of bed? You are the very one God wants to speak to right now to take you to the place of totally depending upon Him and trusting Him with your every need. *You must choose to start trusting God rather than people.*

When parents try to give their children everything they want and continue to try to meet their needs and desires long into adulthood, they are crippling their adult children for life. They are also showing God by their actions that they do not trust Him to meet their children's needs.

Adult children, on the other hand, can use manipulation to get their way and use the tactic of pity parties to get what they want out of parents, which is also sin. This shows a complete lack of trust in God and immaturity as well. We must all grow up! I am not saying at some time when there is a legitimate need that it is sin to help, but as a lifestyle it is clearly wrong.

God wants to *open your eyes* to His well of provision just like Hagar saw in the middle of her desert. God not only wants you to have provision but also He wants you to be in peace. He tells us in His Word, "You will keep in perfect peace those whose minds are steadfast, because they trust in you" (Isaiah 26:3, NIV). Let's take a look at this same verse in another translation of the Bible. The Bible says, "You will keep him in perfect peace, Whose mind is stayed on You, Because he trusts in You" (Isaiah 26:3, NKJV). As we trust in the Lord, pray, and renew our minds, we find that our emotions do not run wild but rather, we have a calm assurance that God will provide in every area as we wait upon Him.

Not only does God keep us in peace as we keep our minds stayed on Him, but He also provides food. The psalmist tells us, "I have never seen the righteous forsaken or their children begging for bread" (Psalm 37:25). The

Lord can move on someone's heart to bring you a meal or provide for you in some manner you least likely expect.

Several months ago, I remember I was at an appointment and the doctor was running late. I had a lunch appointment scheduled, and knew I was not going to have time, so I called and cancelled. I knew if I didn't get a little something to eat that I would have a headache. I thought I could just drive over to the bagel place and get a toasted bagel for a snack. Just in front of the door, a lady dressed in a warm-up suit asked me if I had some change. I told her I would get some inside. I walked inside and the Holy Spirit spoke to my heart to ask her to join me and buy her lunch. I walked back outside and asked her, so we both proceeded through the door. We began to have casual conversation in the line, and I asked her what she would like, so we ordered and I paid for it. We sat down and I prayed over our meal, and then she began to tell me she was homeless due to several bad choices. She expressed that she had a good job but lost it due to falling back into some sin and not getting to work on time. I asked her if she knew Jesus, and she said she had heard about Him. I asked her if I could pray with her and we did. I told her about my appointment and how the Lord had prompted me to come to the bagel place. I gave her money for food and a hotel for the night. She told me she stayed off Sugar Creek Road. I felt so sorry for her and wished I could have done more, but I had to get back to my appointment. On my drive home, the Lord spoke to my heart to go and get a pedicure. Now I can guess that some of you might be thinking now, "Why would God tell her to get a pedicure?" or "Sure, God would do that, right!" He will give you a strange instruction to give you what you need. "Whatever He says to you, do it" (John 2:5)!

I prayed for the young lady on my drive and felt this overwhelming burden for her as I drove. I made it to the nail salon off exit 28 and sat down in the pedicure chair. We always talk—imagine that! The owner normally always has the television on and so it was. This man sharing on the news caught my attention as he began to tell his story. He had been homeless many years before and had started a ministry to house the homeless that would be opening the very next day off *Sugar Creek Road*, the area where this lady stayed near herself. He shared about the churches coming together in the area to help him, and I saw that God answered my prayer to let me know He had provided for tomorrow for this precious woman.

Now, you may not be homeless, but in your heart, you may feel the same. All alone in this big world! However, just as God provided for that lady's day, He is providing for you. I don't know all the details, but He does.

He provides for our needs because He says so in His Word. The apostle Paul says, "My God will meet all your needs according to his glorious riches in Christ Jesus" (Philippians 4:19, NIV) and I believe Him. Jesus told His followers not to worry about what they would eat or drink or wear, but to seek His kingdom first and His righteousness, and then all other things would fall into place (Matthew 6:33).

God provides comfort as we walk through the desert. Our God is described as the *Father of compassion and the God of all comfort who comforts us in all our troubles.* I remember how the Lord comforted me and my family when my dad passed away in January of 2010. God walked with us through that difficult place of grief and sorrow.

Before my daddy passed away, one morning as I awoke, the Holy Spirit whispered to my heart to look under our bed. My husband was already up, so I got up and knelt down beside our bed. I noticed the sun glistening on something, and it was an unopened CD. It had a picture of a little boy on it that looked like my daddy as a kid. He was looking upward. The title was *Hungry Alive.* I told my husband I guess the Lord sent an angel on a special assignment to deliver the CD as there is nothing under our bed. I opened the CD to prepare and listen on my drive back to The Cancer Center in High Point, North Carolina. My phone kept ringing, so I was unable to listen to all the words and the songs as I was informing friends and relatives about Daddy. When I arrived at the hospital, my mom was so excited to have Daddy share what happened the night before. The Lord had opened my daddy's eyes and given him a vision while he was awake. I remember Mom saying, "Your dad had a dream" and Dad quickly corrected saying, "No, I was awake." He began to share how he looked out the window of The Cancer Center and saw a field of white lights.

I will never forget the minute he told me about it. My heart sank and I began to remember the movie *Field of Dreams.* I sensed that the Lord was giving my daddy a glimpse of heaven. The Bible tells us that the Holy Spirit will show us all hidden truth and things to come. (Study John 14–16.) As I left the hospital that day, I stayed off the phone and listened to the CD as I drove home. The first song I heard had lyrics about walking the field of white lights, and my heart was overwhelmed by the love of God, that He would place in my hands something to help me through this desert place. You see, God had shown my daddy the field of white lights, and God Himself had the CD placed under our bed so I could hear the same words on the song. God always confirms His Word and prepares us. *No one, I mean absolutely no one, could orchestrate all these events but God!*

My precious husband gave me the gift of staying at a nearby inn in High Point. I was driving back and forth and spending much time on the road, so this was a huge blessing to spend extra time in prayer with the Lord and be with my parents during this difficult season. My husband would drive over after work each day.

I remember the Lord woke me up one morning and had me look at a particular page in a prayer book I keep with me. The page read, "Comfort for a Person Who Has Lost a Christian Loved One" (*Prayers That Avail Much*).[1] Now I have to say I did not particularly like that page, but I knew that God was showing me what was coming so I could depend on Him and prepare for what was ahead. God walked through this season with us and gave us the most beautiful seventeen days where we surrounded Daddy and did not leave his side before he passed from this life to heaven to be with the Lord. You can read the entire story in my book, *My Father's Heart: How God Walks with Us Through the Valleys.* You can see God's comfort and His amazing love exhibited in my life through the way He showed me things to come to be prepared.

He also gave us the gift of time because on one of the days in the hospital, Daddy was not waking up after a surgical procedure. I was headed to a church meeting that Saturday morning and sensed a sudden urgency in my spirit to go to the hospital instead. Immediately, I turned around and headed back to our home. I called the head of the ladies ministry to inform her and asked her to pray as well. My husband and I headed out toward the hospital immediately, and I called my mom hearing the panic in her precious voice. She told us Daddy was not waking up, so they paged a code and asked her to step outside. Dan and I joined hands and prayed, asking God to raise Daddy up so we could spend time with him. We prayed against the spirit of death and declared, "He shall live and not die and declare all the miracles in his life" (Psalm 118:17). After this happened, I began staying in High Point closer to the hospital.

God answered our prayer by raising Daddy up and giving us the gift of more precious time with him. You can see through these few shared moments of the last days with my daddy, the awesome goodness and love of our heavenly Father! He wants to comfort you as well. God never lies! He is no respecter of persons. What He has done for me, He will do for you. He is our comforter. He went out of His way to show His hand in our lives and walked with us through this valley.

CHAPTER 23

GOD CARES DEEPLY ABOUT THE DETAILS

Love and Mercy

Just as God cared deeply for our entire family during the last days of my daddy's life here on earth, He exhibited His care for Hagar and Ishmael. The Bible tells us, "God was with the boy as he grew up" (Genesis 21:20, NIV). I am sure you will be able to receive comfort just as I did, and just as Hagar did, as you begin to trust God for His provision in every area of your life. He cares deeply about the details in your life and mine.

I was raised in a Christian home and have a wonderful family. I first walked to the altar as a little girl to accept the Lord. After graduation from school, I had great challenges and emotions were tremendous. I walked through divorce, marital abuse, abandonment, betrayal, cancer, and fatality car accidents...yet witnessed the unfailing love and mercy of God.

I did not fully understand that God cared about the details of my life. I have since experienced God's unfailing compassion exhibited in my life on a daily basis as I began to seek Him with my whole heart. I knew there was more, but I did not know how to develop my relationship with my heavenly Father. As I cried out to my God for wisdom, God Himself began to teach me.

I found out God wanted all the details of my life. As I submitted to His Word and authority, God took all the details, straightened them out, and empowered me to live under His direction ever since. He loves us with an everlasting love (Jeremiah 31:3). God has a great plan for your life too (Jeremiah 29:11)!

He took my life and turned it around so I could step into His plan for my life. He called me and chose me before I was formed in my mother's womb. He has brought me before ambassadors of nations and leaders, to sending me to minister to a group of children in the rain forest in Belize. He sent my husband and me to India to minister to pastors where we were invited into the home of government leaders.

The Lord had already prepared me and told me this would happen. He had spoken to my heart one Sunday morning at the beach to stay in the room instead of going to church. If you thought about that for long, your mind would begin to reason. Just obey!

While we were watching Christian television, the Bible that God had instructed me to purchase and take as a gift was being advertised at half price that day. I called to order it, and it arrived just before our trip to India. The Lord had also specifically spoken to my heart to take a particular book as well. God knew exactly how to get the Bible in my hands before the trip. He also knew exactly what items to give this government leader!

Learn to trust Him for everything and obey His instructions. This is just one small portion of how God will give a small instruction for something He has planned in the future. Learn to step out and obey at the slightest whisper from God. God knew what Bible and what book would bless this leader's life in India.

The enemy wanted to cripple me so I would not step into God's plan for my life. God takes broken lives and delights in showing Himself strong on our behalf. He created us in His image and we are special. He created us for purpose and on purpose! Learn to trust God's plan for your life and never give up.

CHAPTER 24

TOTAL TRUST

Seek God's Wisdom

Even after we learn to trust God fully and submit to His precious Word, we will still have times where we face difficult circumstances. It is then when we lean on God and keep our eyes fixed on Him for He is the only one who can take care of any situation and turn it around for our good and His glory. He will empower you with His strength as you trust Him. He is a good God. He is a good Father.

When we face difficult seasons, we must choose to pray:

> *Lord, teach me what I need to learn through this and make me like You. I ask You to help me with my attitude and keep my heart pure and tender toward You. I ask You to give me Your eyes to see through and Your ears to hear with. Don't allow me to miss one instruction, and help me keep my focus on Your plan for my life. Lord, give me a teachable spirit and a tender heart with pure motives.*

God will answer your prayer.

GOD'S CONSTANT PROVISION

God always provides! My mother phoned me to share how God was providing again. Since my mother is a widow now, she was telling me just this last week that she had begun to be concerned about how she was going to take care of the huge lawn and field. God never ceases to amaze me. My first cousin called Mother to tell her that Jeff, her husband, told her not to worry about the lawn for he would take care of the mowing each Saturday this summer. God cares about the natural details in our life, even of maintenance, and always provides. He never ceases to amaze me.

We just have to trust Him! God cares about the fields in life. The fields with harvest are a type and shadow of souls that lie beneath the soil like precious buried treasure that God wants to save for all eternity. You and I are precious gems in the hand of our God. We are a royal diadem. No man and no demon can pluck us out of our heavenly Father's hand.

"How do I know where to start where I am currently?" you might be asking. Pray and seek God. Study the Word of God. Connect yourself with other believers. Trust God, not only for provision, but also for detailed instruction in life. Seek God's wisdom. Read the book of Proverbs. Learn from others who have walked through pain. That is wisdom.

CHAPTER 25

WISDOM FOR WIVES

Encourage and Pray for Your Husband

Women, pray for your husbands! Pray that God will make you so much like Him that your husband is unable to resist you and the God in you. Commit your marriage to God. Don't try to play the Holy Spirit in your husband's life. There is no man alive who will appreciate "holy spirit junior." When you put your expectations in God and not in man, you will never be disappointed (1 Peter 2:6).

Pray Malachi 2:6 over your husband: "No lying can be found in his lips, no unrighteousness can be found in him. He walks in peace with God and turns many others away from iniquity." When you pray God's Word over your husband, the Word will bring change, and angels are dispatched from heaven to minister (Psalm 103:20).

Learn to praise your husband as well. God gives us wisdom in His Word where he instructs us to think on "whatever is true, whatever is noble, whatever is right, whatever is pure, whatever is lovely, whatever is admirable—if anything is excellent or praiseworthy—think about such things" (Philippians 4:8, NIV).

Look for ways to compliment your husband. Find something to praise him about. Tell him you love him, and leave him notes to find later throughout his day. God wants us to speak well of our husband and be good to him.

Pray with other women, but use wisdom when sharing personal, intimate information. Find a trusted counselor, mentor, or leader. You can share too much with the wrong people! Share the details with God. If you live with an unbeliever, you definitely need other believers around for support.

If you are a man, pray with other men. Find a trusted Christian friend and learn to be accountable with someone. If you don't have a Christian friend, ask God to bring you one. He hears and answers prayer.

On a lighter note, men don't always want to hear all the details. Most men like the "bottom line." There are some things that women can share better with other women. It is essential to be connected with other people. God created us for relationship.

Whether you are a man or woman, your spouse will notice your spiritual growth in God and will begin to see the difference God can make in one's life. This will sometimes make them angry, but they will move to the point of being curious for themselves. Ask God to give you a gentle and quiet spirit. Ask God to give you a heart to hear what your spouse is saying.

God can use our trials to exhibit His strength in us for others to see when we walk through difficult times. Women tend to grow faster spiritually than men. Men think more rationally, so I believe that is why they sometimes grow at a slower pace. When change does not come quickly, women can have a tendency to jump in and help God out. God doesn't need that kind of help. We must remind ourselves that only God can bring change. When we focus on changing ourselves through God, we will be able to surrender others to Him.

Learn to show respect for your husband. He needs respect. Learn to allow your husband time to get through the door and reconnect with him before sharing problems of the day. When you show him unconditional respect, it makes him feel like your prince. This, in turn, will motivate him to show love and honor you as his princess. Where there is no respect, there is no order. Where there is no order, there is chaos and conflict.

Keep in mind that together your marriage is a reflection of God's love on earth. Realizing that both men and women need love and respect will open the door for you to desire to meet the desire of his heart's deepest cry: respect. *When he senses your respect, he will do anything to show his love for you.* Look to your husband with love and adoration, realizing how you treat your husband is a reflection of your relationship with God. It is our training ground. Remembering the mind is the battlefield will encourage you to greatly seek God with your whole heart, renew your mind faithfully through the Word of God, and seek above all else to be the best wife you can be to meet your husband's needs. Ask God to help you be the wife your husband needs.

You can learn a lot about a famous person on the newest sources of connection such as Face Book, Twitter, etc., but you never really get to know the person. For instance, you could have been raised in the church and learned a lot about God but not know Him yourself. We really get to know our spouse through the years of marriage when we learn to communicate. We are all different, and we all have different body languages. People see things differently. We each have different personality types, and it is crucial for both to recognize that both are different in outlook, perspective, and bodily function. We are able to see more quickly what is being done *to us* before we can clearly see what we are doing *to our spouse.*

A MAN'S WORK

When you begin to realize how important a man's work is to him, you will then be willing to take the step of showing honor and respect, which are extremely vital to him. Honor and respect are more important to a man than love. A man has a natural desire to "hunt and conquer" the world and work to achieve. God created man this way.

When we praise our husband for being a good provider, we build him up and show honor and respect. He also needs empathy when things are going wrong at work. This will enable him to work harder for the desired end result, as his lifelong goal is to be a great provider for his wife and family. He needs the support of his wife, even when he has made mistakes.

When a man tries to "run the roost" and ignores suggestions from his wife, he is walking down a path of destruction. He is showing disrespect for his wife and destroying her feeling of security, which she so greatly needs. Without security there can be a lack of intimacy.

If a husband's wife criticizes his work, he feels disrespected. Many times, a man that grew up in an environment without the approval of his mom or dad, or was called such things as "the black sheep of the family," will oftentimes hear what his wife says as confirmation, over and over again, of what he heard as a child growing up. This solidifies the belief and can cause him to lose hope, have a broken spirit, and no will to strive to be diligent. The enemy knows our weaknesses and sets us up to be upset. Men are highly sensitive in this area, so any put-downs are heard as criticism.

Since a man's job is also to protect his wife, he carries the umbrella protection given to him by God for her and his family. It is his responsibility and not his right. The Bible tells women that a gentle and quiet spirit will win her husband over. The key to empowering people is by giving them what they want, so they in turn give you what you need because they get to do so. When you respect your husband in the area of work and surrender to his protection, he feels like the "big man" or the prince of his home, and will lay his life down for his woman. He will look for ways to please his wife.

CHAPTER 26

WISDOM FOR HUSBANDS

Listen to and Pray for Your Wife

Take time to listen to what your wife is saying from her heart. The key to energizing your marriage is by meeting your spouse's most heartfelt need. It will be different for every couple. Ask God for His wisdom. Put down the telephone or laptop or whatever kind of latest "gizmo" you have and talk to your wife. Take her to dinner and hold her hand. Hold her hand when she is going down the stairs. Open her car door and let her know she is the most important person in your life. Love her by showing her respect and honor her opinions. Love and honor are like a breath of fresh air to your marriage! Make time for each other, and learn to have fun together. These tips will help improve your marriage.

A fun weekend getaway or a marriage workshop will enhance and improve your marriage. It doesn't mean your marriage is in trouble, it is just a great place to learn that everyone goes through seasons in marriage. Marriage is work but it can be fun. Relationships are work. To have a successful, vibrant marriage, you have to make it your priority.

God will sometimes use your wife to give you wisdom even in your business or profession, and in most cases, the last person your natural flesh wants to hear a suggestion from is your wife. Am I right, guys?

How many times has your wife said something like, "Why don't we stop for directions?" but instead, you drive for endless hours out of the way, secretly wishing you had listened to your wife and actually taken the advice. Well, if that's you, you are not alone. That is life!

I remember early on when Dan and I were first married, we had an issue. Have any of you experienced an issue? We had purchased a new washer and dryer and were giving the set we had to someone in our family. I remember saying to my husband, "Why don't you wait until Brad gets here so he can help you?" and Dan got angry. I didn't like his tone of voice to me but later began to understand that what he really thought I was saying was that he was not capable of moving the washer and dryer himself. I just thought it would be safer and less of a load to carry with help, especially carrying it out to the garage and down the stairs.

We can laugh about it now, but it taught us a valuable lesson. Do you see how things can be misconstrued? Men and women hear differently.

The Bible says, "Each one of you also must love his wife as he loves himself, and the wife must respect her husband" (Ephesians 5:33, NIV). Remember this! How you treat your wife all day long is how she will respond to you in the evening. Don't say things you will later regret. Ask God what it is like to live with you through your wife's eyes. You might be surprised at what God shows you!

Ask God to change you and make you the best husband your wife needs. Ask God to change you to have a heart like His. I promise you that He will answer that prayer.

CHAPTER 27

GOD'S TIMING

Is Not Our Timing

God's timing is often not our timing. God's way is normally not our way or plan of action either. There is no life that God can't transform. Don't ever say, "A person will never change" or "There is no hope for them" because there is always hope in God. The Holy Spirit is the one who brings change. There is no life that is beyond His power to save and restore. Don't ever give up on anyone, just give them to God. God is the only one who can reach people, and He knows exactly when and where that will occur. God's arm is not too short to save (Isaiah 59:1). All things are possible with God. (See Matthew 19:26.)

Stop saying, "God can't change someone's heart" and begin to agree with God's Word over their life. Ask God to forgive you for speaking negatively over everyone and that includes yourself. If you are reading this now, God has not written you off either. He has a plan for you. He didn't write me off, but instead, He wrote my name in the Lamb's Book of Life for all eternity when I accepted Him. He has a plan for everyone. We just have to choose His plan and walk in His Word.

God is wiser than all. He knows the end from the beginning! Since He created the universe, don't you think He is capable? He honors His Word. Pray His Word over your life and family. Watch God at work in your life and your family's life. Get your focus back on God and not on demanding to see it now. You will begin to notice you are growing, and time spent in prayer is never wasted when you surrender to God's time and plan.

Let's take a glance at an example in the Bible. We find that Paul rejected John Mark for a mission trip because the younger man had deserted Paul in Acts 15:37–39. Yet, years later Paul requested John Mark's companionship in 2 Timothy 4:11. Sometimes we are not waiting on God, He is waiting on us. We are all in training. As with John Mark, if we don't pass a test, God keeps giving us the test over and over again until we understand what He wants to teach us. There are things we must know to be prepared for everything in life. God knows best how to prepare and protect us for the future, and He is our rear guard too!

Don't become weary in waiting on God. Keep doing what God has spoken to your heart to do. You will begin to notice His hand in every area of your life and every trial you walk through. God is always with us, and His timing is perfect.

CHAPTER 28

WE ARE A TEAM WITH GOD

Honor God First

Women sometimes show disrespect for their husband's suggestions, thinking they don't have the right to tell them anything or have no right to share their insight. Oftentimes, God will use our husband to share something with us that we need to know, change, or redirect. Most women do not want to hear the advice from their husband until they realize they are a team. When a woman hears a suggestion and it is not given in a harsh manner, but shows genuine concern, she will respond with thankfulness.

Body language is vitally important in the marriage. We sometimes say more with our body language than with our words. Men and women think differently. When a woman says she has nothing to wear, it really means she doesn't have anything new. On the other hand, when a man says he has nothing to wear, he is letting you know what he wanted to wear is dirty or the laundry has piled up. The process of becoming one is sometimes painful and a little bit like walking on eggshells at times. However, once we get there and fully know our spouse is with us for life and shares God's value of the covenant of marriage, we can move through anything in life together as a team with God as the head of our home.

As we aspire to inspire others through this journey we call life, we must perspire and respire. *Respire* is to inhale and exhale air for the purpose of maintaining life.[1] Jesus is the air we breathe. When we learn to abide in Him as one together and separately as individuals, we learn to grow together at a much faster pace. We reach the place where we desire to please our heavenly Father and each other. We love life and look at situations differently. *Respire* also means to breath freely again after anxiety, trouble, etc. Have you ever experienced trouble? I know I have. *Respiration* is "the sum total of the physical and chemical processes in an organism by which oxygen is conveyed to tissues and cells and the oxidation products, carbon dioxide and water, are given off."[2]

Sometimes people have to wear an oxygen mask or use a respirator for life. My daddy had to use a Bi-Pap machine to help him breathe before he passed from this life to heaven. When a person's body begins to fail in this area, eventually they will die unless they use life support of some kind.

In the same token, many people, and some Christians, are not breathing in the life of God. God desires that we aspire to inspire others to come to know Him as well. They may be in the middle of a desert, and you are the well of living water that God has cleverly positioned near them to help them walk through to healing.

The word *aspire* means "to be eagerly desirous, especially, for something great or of high value."[3] One can aspire to be a doctor or aspire to grow spiritually. It takes aspiration to make a choice, and it takes a corresponding action to achieve an end result.

Inspire means "to infuse an animating, quickening, or exalting influence into." It also means "to produce or arouse; to influence or impel" (opposition can inspire us to a greater effort).[4] As I was sitting in a worship service several months ago, I heard the Lord say to me, *"Aspire to inspire others."* Never quit. Then, I began to hear Him saying, *"Aspire, inspire, respire, perspire."* I realize that we have to work up a sweat to perspire. Relationships take work. *Perspire* means "to excrete watery fluid through the pores; sweat; to emit through the pores; to blow constantly [said of the wind], to breathe through; to sweat insensibly."[5] We have to choose to have a great relationship and work at it daily with God's help.

EXPERIENCING MORE OF GOD

When your spouse does not aspire to grow spiritually, you must not allow his or her lack of desire to prevent you from getting to know God and worship at His throne. You must choose to keep your heart focused on God rather than on a need you see in your mate. You must choose to focus on your own personal growth with the Lord, especially, in the midst of any storm or desert. When you feel alone, you must realize you are never alone because He is always present. He always hears our heart's cry.

Today, I was telling the Lord about our ministry and the books I am working on diligently. I asked the Lord to please give me a word of encouragement to make sure I am on the right track. We all need encouragement and must be willing to ask for it as well.

My husband had a short board meeting right after the service, so I sat with my nephew, mother, and sister on the pew and waited. A lady came up to me and said she had something God wanted her to share with me. She told me God said that He had doors opened for me and He had cleared the path. She continued to say that He was well pleased with me and I was in His timing. This was confirmation of God hearing and answering my prayer.

I had expressed my desire to the Lord and kept moving forward with life. As my husband and I were standing praying for others, God illuminated me to this precious lady and gave her His word for me. As you continue to stay planted, keep praying and encouraging others, God Himself will encourage you as well.

God let me know I was definitely not alone in worship. You can worship, whether standing in the midst of a church service, in your car, or in the privacy of your own home. Worship starts in the heart. Being alone with God even in the midst of thousands is like standing in the presence of God with your own private audience. He makes His ways known to us in the most exciting and personal ways. Living in the Spirit and seeing God's hand in the details becomes a natural way of life.

Instead of focusing on worshiping the Lord while you are in church, you might be thinking, "Is my husband or wife catching what the pastor is saying? Why isn't my spouse holding my hand this morning?" Worship is not about who is beside you, it is about your personal walk with the Lord and your focus on Him. Not only is it about your focus on Him, but the fact that you know and recognize His focus on you as well. What an amazing revelation. We team up with God by keeping Him as our focus.

SHATTERED DREAMS AFTER A BROKEN HEART

If you have a broken heart and feel like your dreams have been shattered, once again, it is the time to prepare to experience the kind of love you are looking for in the future. As you allow God to bring healing to your heart, while you renew your mind through His Word, you will find that you will desire a mate that has a strong spiritual life in God. Your mind remembers the negative and positive affirmations, the pain, and collects the trash in life and the grains of sand from opinions of others while walking through the desert. Have you ever had sand in your shoes? It makes it uncomfortable to walk. It is the same when we keep the opinions of others in front of what God says—we are unable to walk victoriously.

Choosing to renew your mind to the truth of God's Word on a daily basis is the key to change within you. The water of God's Word is like a stream or a well in the desert where we find refreshing and the quench to our thirst. The Bible says, "That he might sanctify and cleanse it with the washing of water by the word" (Ephesians 5:26).

When both are connected to God and put Him first, the physical aspect and emotional aspect of marriage is far better and more fulfilling.

There are always pain and consequences to wrong choices. But God still has a great plan through the desert of broken hearts and shattered dreams. As we choose to worship God in the good times and in the bad, our perspective changes. We find that the broken places in our hearts begin to heal.

We must choose to honor God above all else and focus on maturing in our spiritual life. When both the husband and wife honor God first, they go through the process of becoming one in God. This is where transparency and freedom come to share your deepest secrets, your unspoken dreams, and to express your heartfelt emotions. You arrive at the place of knowing your mate cares about the details in your life. He or she is the one you look to as your best friend, lover, and partner in life. With God at the center of marriage, and both working for the common goal, any marriage relationship can thrive and be a happy union.

CHAPTER 29

PRAYER AND WORSHIP

Preparation

W e can also be wounded by people in organizations. I found myself wounded and hurt by a few church people many years ago (as a teenager) when they made it evident I was not as holy as they were because I was raised Methodist and did not have the same religious beliefs as that church. The pastor preached on demons and what not to wear, and where not to go, and what not to say. I felt like God had this huge baseball bat and was just waiting for me to mess up to wipe me out clean. I remember feeling like I did not fit in at all. I am so thankful God had a little elderly grandmother there that loved me and prayed with me. She was just precious. She was genuine and made great biscuits too. She warmly invited me into the family of God and made sure I knew God had a *great* plan for my life. I still think about her. She encouraged me to be everything God wanted me to be and to aspire to dream big. I'll never forget her. She's in heaven now.

You can be bruised or wounded in church by people, because where there are people, there will be problems. The enemy will try to get you offended at leadership, authority figures, and the people that have the ability to help you. You must choose to forgive, keep going to church, and find His plan for your life. He is the ultimate teacher. God has a master plan for you.

Whether you are single, married, divorced, widowed, or find yourself in the middle of a church battle between leadership, remember this, God says in His Word that He will turn everything out for our ultimate good and His glory. I look back now on my painful experiences and realize God used those to teach me how to love people who are downtrodden in life and feel left out.

Let's take a look at Hannah in the Bible for a minute. Hannah knew well what it meant to worship alone as she spent time in the temple pouring her heart out to God and crying for a child. The priest thought she was drunk, but Hannah still respected him, and God turned the situation around for her good and God's glory. God blessed her with a child that she in turned committed to God.

At a time in history when infertility earned a woman both scorn, shame, and ridicule, Hannah faced heartache at the hand of her husband's other wife. Had you been Hannah, how would you have responded? Do you find yourself today in a blended family and disputes hindering your worship with God? Is your heart bruised or do you feel alone in your desert?

Hannah refused to lash out at her rival, but instead turned to God and poured out her sorrow and loss to Him. She still honored the man of God. She earnestly prayed and worshiped God, but persistently begged him for a son. She prayed sincerely, even when openly rebuked by an uncomprehending priest. God rewarded her faith with a son, Samuel. She kept her word and gave Samuel to the Lord with a thankful heart (1 Samuel 1:1–28). Prayer changed the course of Hannah's life and impacted an entire nation. Even though Hannah found herself in the midst of the desert of ridicule and heartache, she continued to worship God. God used her son in a key role as a prophet during the lifetime of King David. Samuel's influence outlived him as he left a legacy of his influence toward the prophetic movement. God also blessed Hannah with many other children. This shows the power of persistence in having the heart of a worshiper even in the midst of a bruised heart and difficult circumstances.[1]

PREPARED TO HEAR

Worship is personal, passionate, and prepares our hearts to hear God. As I think back over my own life, I remember sweet times the Lord has spoken to my heart. I remember the opening of my eyes to see Him in the spirit standing at the pulpit at our church now. It was during worship. The Lord whispered to my heart, "Read Psalm 63:2," so I immediately sat down and turned to the page in my Bible to the passage where I read, "I saw the Lord in the sanctuary." What a confirmation. God was speaking to me personally. He is still speaking today! Do you hear Him? Have you prepared your heart to hear Him?

Pastor Rick, the lead pastor at our church, had a vision that same week as well. He saw the Lord standing in front of the pulpit. Jesus opened His robe back to reveal the leeches on the body of Christ. This represented the need for cleansing for the body of Christ, God's people. God was confirming that the entire body of Christ globally is in need of a cleansing before His return.

When we walk through seasons of **pain**, we are positioned and aligned in need of God. We need His cleansing so we may become more like Him. We must choose to stay connected to God and church in the good times and the difficult. We are not to forsake the assembling together with other believers for corporate worship (Hebrews 10:25). We also can't live off Sunday morning worship services alone either. We are unable to survive on one meal a week, so how could we survive and thrive with one message a week? Worship must flow from our personal lives, whether in the privacy of our own home or driving down the road worshiping in our car.

In Psalm 18, we read where David recalls how he called to the Lord, and the Lord heard his voice (See Psalm 18:3–6). You can see how David experienced the Lord's goodness firsthand. He knew the Lord as his rock, fortress, deliverer, shield, salvation, and stronghold. David could worship God due to his own personal experiences with God. How about you? Do you have your own personal experience with God? When was the last time you experienced a fresh encounter with God? You will be able to worship God alone when you have your own worship encounters with Him alone in the desert. We sometimes find our worship stems from an extended time in the desert. What desert place have you found yourself in now?

Worship is a passionate experience. Praise begins to flow from your heart. You wake each morning with a song in your heart toward God. Have you said like David, "I desire nothing more than you Lord" (Psalm 27:4)? David desired to be up close and personal with God. Do you? As you move your focus toward God and desire to have a face-to-face encounter with Him, you will find yourself in worship and heartfelt praise. Passion for God and worship of God will flow from a heart centered on God.

God clarified some plans in my life today through a lady I have only met once who heard God and stepped out immediately in obedience. That's the love of God. How many times do you think we miss hearing God or miss hearing the confirmation due to being too busy, or having our hearts improperly prepared to hear Him? It is in the desert places that we learn to hear God at a higher level. God sometimes chooses to speak a word to us when we are alone and quiet where we can actually hear what He is saying.

God also wants us to worship with others. As important as it is to seek God on our own in a time of worship, it is vitally important to connect with others as well. He desires us to be comfortable being alone with Him without the distraction of others. We must learn to worship as if no one else were in the room. We must also learn to connect with others.

DEPENDENCE ON GOD

When we place our trust in God, we will not experience failure and disappointment in God. Man will fail us, but God will not. Our relationship with God is strengthened in the desert because we learn to depend on God and not on man. It is not until one experiences the heartache or rejection in the desert that we fully understand and know our value in God's eyes. Do you have patience to wait on God for His plan and answers, or do you give God deadlines and want to control others? Sometimes God leads us into the desert so we can learn to depend on Him.

What about you? Have you learned to depend on Him? Is time spent with Him more precious than anything else? When we learn by personal experience that God cares about the details in our lives, praise will be the overflow of our heart.

GOD IS THE LOVER OF MY SOUL

Worship is about Jesus. It has nothing to do with my outward appearance but has everything to do with my heart. I must worship in humility, thankfulness, and from a heart of adoration. The Bible tells us in Psalm 95:6, "Come, let us bow down in worship," which represents a heart of humility and adoration for the Lord. He loves you and me. We can worship by getting on our knees or standing with our arms outstretched toward heaven. When you truly worship and fall in love with Jesus, you begin to recognize He is the lover of your soul.

Psalm 100:2 says to worship God with gladness. Sometimes I sing in the car, and I am thankful when I get to heaven, I will have a better singing voice. It is not about how I sound to my neighbor, but the purity of my heart before the Lord in total abandonment of worshiping Him.

In Matthew 15:9 Jesus warned about "people [who] honor me with their lips but their hearts are far from me." He said, "They worship me in vain." Defilement comes from within. When you are thinking about what you are going to prepare for lunch or what time the neighbors are coming over, you are worshiping God in vain. If we are totally honest with ourselves, we will admit we have done the same. You can learn to enter God's presence in your mind and heart, even when sitting in a dinner function with people all around. Worship becomes a way of life.

God is not limited to how He speaks to us, provides for us, or ministers to us. He is not restricted by anything. You can be at a conference and sitting in your hotel room and hear the voice of God, noticing a bumper sticker that totally confirms God's Word to you, or taking your Bible out and hearing the Lord whisper a verse for you to read.

God goes out of His way to let us know He is present. He goes out of His way to show us His path of righteousness. We have choices to make, and sometimes we don't make the right choices. Then, when we find ourselves in the midst of a mess, we want God to bless our mess. He promises to help us when we repent. Has He been calling out to you?

Sometimes, God calls us to come away with Him, just to spend time with Him alone. It can be in the midst of a chaotic day to a short getaway that you plan just to hear from God. It can be in the carpool line picking up your kids or in the bathroom getting ready for the new day. When you hear something that reminds you of Him, take time to worship Him and tell Him you love Him. Have you become too occupied with the cares of the world or your own personal desert to come away with Him? Perhaps it is even the Holy Spirit that led you there just so you could come to know Jesus, the Lover of your soul.

Set goals of spending time with Him and daily disciplines. Learn to practice the presence of God wherever you are. You will be glad you did. He is calling out to you today, Jesus, the Lover of your soul. He goes to extreme measures to warn us and save us from harm. He goes to extreme measures to spend time with us! Learn to create memories by spending time with Him. We create memories when we spend time with people. Spend time with family and create your own memories that will last long after your beloved family has passed from this life to heaven. Don't say things you will regret long after they are gone. Learn to speak life and love now, before it is too late!

MONUMENTS OF REMEMBRANCE

When people pass away, their loved ones normally place a monument or headstone at the grave site. This is to mark the place of burial. All through the Bible, we find where altars were built to mark a specific place of trial and breakthrough. When we lose someone to death, it is very hard, especially if it was a sudden death. I know with my father's recent passing, God gave us the most beautiful gift of spending much time with him prior to his death. I have been to the grave site to honor him, but know he is not there. His body was placed in the grave. God spoke to me to do something very interesting the day of his funeral.

At the funeral home, I gave a cousin's wife one of my bookmarks with my contact information on it and how God cares about the details in each of our lives. I was out of business cards, and my mom had one of the bookmarks in her purse. The funeral director had given us stationery with envelopes and seals for anyone who wanted to write a letter to Daddy to place in the casket. On the day of the funeral, the Holy Spirit spoke to my heart to place one of my bookmarks in the envelope and seal it with seven seals. I remembered the day before the Lord spoke a scripture to my heart about how everything has to die and be placed in the ground to bring forth life. I know the Lord has spoken to my heart that He has us and the ministry in His right hand.

I prepared the envelope with the seven seals and placed it in my purse. When the funeral director picked us up for the funeral, I asked him if he would mind placing something in Daddy's casket. I spoke at my daddy's funeral, and after the service as we were headed back home, I wondered if the funeral director placed the envelope with Daddy, so I asked him. I'll never forget the look in his eyes as I could see them in the rearview mirror as he was driving us in the funeral car. He asked me, "Do you mind telling me who that was from?" so I told him it was from me. Then he asked if I minded telling him what it was. I began to share the series of events and how God told me our ministry was in His right hand. As tears swelled up in his eyes, he proceeded to share how he had tried two or three times to open the drawer inside the casket but it would not open, so he placed the envelope in my daddy's right hand. Wow! What an amazing God! It gets better too!

The very next day, not even twenty-four hours later, my cousin's wife called me at Mom's home and proceeded to share how she couldn't sleep and had stayed up all night reading my bookmark. She began to share about her life, and we prayed together on the phone. She asked the Lord to become her Savior less than twenty-four hours after that small step of obedience with the bookmark. That is the power of God. Even though we were walking through the valley due to my daddy's death, God was still at work in the smallest details to *touch one more*. What an amazing God we have the opportunity to serve and worship!

When we choose to commit and lay everything down for the Lord, He will raise it up for His purposes in the earth. Keep your eyes fixed on Christ, stay on the steady course, and remember we are not home yet, but we are on our way too. This is not our eternal home.

CHAPTER 30

FEELING FORSAKEN

Nothing Can Take You from God's Hands

Even though you may feel forsaken at times, feeling forsaken is not the same as being forsaken. Jesus cried out to God from the cross, "And about the ninth hour Jesus cried out with a loud voice, saying, 'Eli, Eli, lama sabachthani?' that is, 'My God, My God, why have you forsaken me?'" (Matthew 27:46). These words were uttered by our Savior from the cross over two thousand years ago, yet you may be feeling the same way today as many others. Even in your trial that left you wandering in the desert of loneliness, your soul may be struggling and feeling forsaken by God too. Perhaps you don't even feel like trusting God or anyone else for that matter. You prayed and prayed and asked God to reveal the truth and to help you keep your marriage together, but no matter what, your husband walked out on you. You may be a man who has been left by your wife for another man, and find yourself with a business and three children to take care of on your own. You may have been driven into a financial desert and have lost all hope. In any case, God has not forsaken you! No matter what you have experienced, there is hope in the cross of Jesus Christ!

Let's take a look at what God said in His Word in the book of John. "In the beginning was the Word, and the Word was with God, and the

Word was God. He was in the beginning with God. All things were made through Him, and without Him nothing was made that was made...And the Word became flesh and dwelt among us, and we beheld His glory, the glory as of the only begotten of the Father, full of grace and truth" (John 1:1–3, 14).

The term "Word" in these passages are all the same Greek word *logos* (Strong's # 3056) to describe the "Word" of God.[1] The Word of God was made flesh in His Son Jesus Christ, who came to earth as a baby and grew up into a man. Jesus Christ isn't just the Word made flesh. He is the Promise(s) of God incarnate. He is Peace. Even though Jesus was the Son of God, He still experienced the feelings of being forsaken by God the Father.

Jesus knew His Father would never leave Him nor forsake Him; however, he still experienced the feelings. He encountered the sin of fallen humanity. We too, can feel forsaken, but it is definitely not the same as being forsaken. You may have experienced that at the hand of a spouse or some other person, but God will never forsake you. You may have lost a partnership in a firm where you have given your all. You may find yourself at the wrong end on a real estate deal that went sour. Whatever the case, God will never forsake you.

The Hebrew word which is most often translated as "forsaken" is *'azab* (pronounced ah-zav; Strong's #5800). The basic meaning is "to leave, abandon, depart from, to let loose [the idea of being loose/not firmly attached], to let go, and to leave behind."[2] God promises you He will never abandon you. You may have been abandoned as a child by a parent, by a spouse, or by a family, but God is still faithful. Beloved, nothing can take you from God's hands.

God is saying to you that He knows what you are feeling. He knows you feel pain of rejection and hurt, but He is still with you. He is crying out to you today, "Come unto Me, all you who are heavy laden and I will give you rest" (Matthew 11:28).

By coming into the Lord's presence and experiencing His love through difficult seasons, we will have the calm assurance that He promises to restore our hope and lives through His Word made flesh and through His promise(s). Memorize the following verse, as it will help you through:

> Be strong and of good courage, do not fear nor be afraid of them;
> for the Lord your God, He is the One who goes with you. He will
> not leave you nor forsake you.
>
> —DEUTERONOMY 31:6

You may be feeling forsaken right now. Your husband may have had another outburst of rage that you have experienced for many years, leaving you with post traumatic stress disorder. You may be thinking, "I thought I would not experience this again, and here we go again." Your spouse may have just walked out the door to have an affair, and he doesn't know you are aware. Your spouse may have committed suicide a few months back and left you with grief, bills, and sadness. Your child may have just left for college, and you feel like your heart is broken. You may feel like the whole world is crumbling in around you. It is at this very place the Lord of lords, and King of kings, Jesus, wants to bring healing to your heart.

LOVE GOD AND LOVE OTHERS

At your lowest point, God is near. He will use your situations to achieve His purpose. He doesn't cause bad things to happen. God is a good God. Learn to outlive your life through small acts of compassion to others while you are walking through the desert. As actions speak louder than words, take the time to look for someone who is hurting. You can tell someone you love them, but the tone of your voice can tell them something different. Be gentle, kind, sensitive, loyal, and forgiving toward others. As you reach out to help someone else, believe it or not, this will help your process go faster. It really takes your focus off your current situation and puts it on helping others.

Even in the midst of your darkest hour, God can use you to help someone else. I remember years ago, every time I would finish a Christian book, the Lord would tell me to give it to someone. He would always position someone with a need, and I would have the perfect book in my hand. That's the way God works.

Obey God's promptings and little nudges at your heart. You may feel you have gotten the short end of a stick or a raw deal; then you are just the person God delights in transforming. God wants you to discover His plan for you even in the chaos. He wants to embrace you with a relationship with Him. He wants you to realize just how precious you are to Him. He wants to heal you so He can reveal the hidden treasures He has placed inside you that He will use to present Jesus to the world. Love people by pointing them to Jesus!

CHAPTER 31

MARRIAGE

Training Ground

Marriage is God's holy covenant and a training ground. You are unable to leave and cleave at the same time. The same occurs as a person continues to focus on his or her past. They are unable to move forward with God's plan for their life. *Rehearse sounds like death to me.* Continually speaking about the pain or rehearsing the past produces death and greater pain. You are unable to cleave to your spouse if you do not cut the cords financially and emotionally with your parents. It is impossible.

Many marriages have failed due to one or both not leaving their parents. Sure, they have left the home, in most cases, but they may have not cut the cords financially or left emotionally. When there is a crisis, who do you run to? Is it Mom or Dad, or is it your spouse? Who is the first person you call?

If your spouse has left you and you are alone now, and you recognize these symptoms, it is not too late to learn and have your life transformed for the future. If your marriage is a little shaky, begin to work on your marriage. Ask God to make you the husband or wife that your spouse needs. Learn your spouse's love language and what they need. What they complain about is vital information they are giving you to help you succeed. You can learn new things, if you are willing.

Let's just suppose the young lady getting married doesn't think her ring is big enough that her fiancé can afford because her parents have always given her exactly what she wanted. It might be the size of their first home to a new dress; either way, if the parents interfere, there will be problems. One or both of her parents may have always come to her rescue and put her first. If her husband has to borrow money from someone or get money from someone as a gift to purchase something he cannot yet afford, you already have signs for a failing marriage. When the young lady doesn't get something she wants in the marriage, she will still run to her parents. The young lady has been spoiled and has false precepts about what marriage actually is based upon. Her husband is in for a world of hurt and will *never* measure up to her parents. Cleaving takes energy, time, and practice. You have to leave before you can cleave.

Becoming one is a blending of all aspects of life, emotionally, physically, and financially. When you move from "I" in the marriage to "us" and "we," you have reached the goal of becoming one where you have a lifelong commitment and covenant with God and your spouse. You have open communication and a willingness to listen to both parties.

When you have a ton of baggage coming into the marriage, the best decision you will ever make is to go through marriage counseling. Problems will arise. Never say the word *divorce* to your mate or threaten leaving. When you do, you summon demonic spirits to attack you to set you up for divorce. The enemy hates marriage and family. He attacks the home.

You may be thinking that is a little extreme, but the spiritual world is real, whether you believe it or not. The enemy does not show up at your front door dressed in a red suit with a pitchfork to announce his plan for your demise. It is the wrong cup of coffee with the opposite sex, the glance that you dwell on way too long that leads to an affair, or the series of wrong choices you are aware you are making when you feel God tugging at your heart and saying, "Don't go there."

REMEMBER ANYTHING OF VALUE TAKES WORK

There is great wisdom and value in going to conferences, marriage counseling, retreats, and working on your marriage. When you love your spouse sacrificially it makes them *feel* loved. Make your home a calm and beautiful place for your wife. Allow her to decorate the home. Men, make sure the lawn is taken care of, either by you or have it maintained. Start reading the Bible with your spouse and pray together. Practice at making your marriage work. You must guard your mind, spirit, and body. Plan to get away with your spouse to spend quality time.

Drawing close to one another, with God as the head, will bring clarity to your marriage. The secret to a lasting relationship is there has to be three in the marriage, God, husband, and wife. Marriage is a *holy covenant* and not a contract. It takes both parties giving 100 percent. It is an agreement and guarantee one person makes with another. Marriage is a promise, has a condition of covenant outlines, is by ratified by blood; and the sign of evidence or token is the ring each wears.

A vital secret is to remember and reflect on your vows frequently. Look at your wedding pictures! Think back to how you felt the week before you were about to be married to your spouse. In Song of Solomon 3:6 we find the wedding was a celebration. Learn to celebrate your marriage.

Let's observe Song of Solomon. Solomon and his procession were fitting only for a king. The wedding should be a time of great joy and celebration. The day is like no other you will experience. The wedding of your youth is the first experience, and you will well remember it. The celebration was pageantry comes as a surprise to many today due to the fact most were more civil and took place in the home rather than in a temple. The procession was led by the groom to his bride's home, and he escorted her back to her new home where the actual wedding took place. The wedding feast that followed sometimes lasted up to an entire week. This was a special ritual where both pledged their love to each other. The pageantry and procession were to honor her and appropriately sanctify her. It was a once in a lifetime event.

The wedding of Prince William and Kate that took place in April of 2011 was an event for the whole world to see on television. You can view this as a type and shadow of our soon coming King Jesus, coming back for his bride to be wed. Jesus is royalty and He has grafted us into His kingdom. What a day that will be!

Secondly, Solomon wanted the world to know how much he loved Shulamite, and he was putting her on parade. The smoke was a result of burning frankincense and myrrh. Frankincense was used often as a source of fire, produced a huge flame, and was used in the temple as a symbol of prayer. This provided a great flame and smoke. This is a picture of our prayers ascending to God. As they came from Shunem to Jerusalem, they had the torches you could see for some distance. Myrrh had a pungent aroma. You could see and smell the aroma. (This is a reminder of our spiritual wedding to Christ as well.) When you decide to get married, you will pray before... and I guarantee that you will afterwards. A wedding should be a statement of the importance of the husband and wife getting married.

The wedding was a time to celebrate the uniqueness of each in the marriage. In marriages today, many use slide presentations starting with baby pictures to their present age and sometimes get quite a laugh from the congregation. Oh, how different the marriage celebration is today. However, they both end up at the altar.

A wedding is a time of certification. When Solomon came for Shulamite, he did not come alone. He brought an army with him. He was letting her know she would be safe with him. Sixty warriors represented one-tenth of his bodyguards. Perhaps the sixty became his friends as he got to know them and as they participated in the event, but their primary duty was to guard the wedding, pledging their lives to protect Solomon and Shulamite. In essence, Solomon was communicating, "You will be safe with me, and you can trust me." I've never been to a wedding where there were sixty armed guards. What an experience that must have been!

Jesus holds a space for us, a place in heaven beside Him. We can give one another shelter. We cannot change the wind and waves, but we can provide a place of safety in each other's arms. We find shelter in each other when we walk through the desert together. When we walk through the storms in life, we form a greater bond that is not easily broken. We give safety to the one we love.

When Solomon was coming back from Shunem with His bride, he had sixty valiant men with swords. Solomon was saying to his precious bride, "You will be safe and *secure*." They were carrying Solomon's couch. His couch was somewhat like a beautiful royal carriage.

On our wedding invitation we had a Cinderella carriage similar with the scripture, "The Lord appeared to us in the past saying: I have loved you with an everlasting love; I have drawn you with unfailing kindness" (Jeremiah 31:3, NIV). The wedding gown I chose was called "Everlasting Love." God says in His Word, "I will build you up again, and you...will be rebuilt" (Jeremiah 31:4, NIV); this Word is for you today! I had failed relationships because I had what I call a "wrong picker" and ended up in the desert of divorce.

God brought me a wonderful husband this time, and we have been married fifteen years. I must tell you that all marriages take work. There are no perfect relationships. However, there is hope after failed relationships. I know personally because I have lived it! The enemy loves to bring up your past. When we are born again and receive God's forgiveness, He removes our past as far as the east is from the west. He rebuilds us as we walk through the pain with Him at our side. The only ones that remember our past are the devil and the people he uses. I wouldn't want to be in either category, would you? When people throw up your past or start pointing fingers, they are usually blame shifting and trying to make themselves look better by belittling someone else.

The military demonstration represented in Song of Solomon 3:8 was with sixty warriors who were not just on parade, they were ready to fight. There was a threat of fear on the journey through the night. They made it evident they wanted Shulamite to feel secure in her new role. God was present with her as she was brought to Jerusalem. (See Spiritual Application/Army of God.)

God has already won the battle and sends His angels to protect and preserve us today. He desires that we love Him with our whole heart. He desires that we learn His Word and come to know Him. He wants us to know we are secure in Him. He desires that we learn how to step out in His authority that He gave us through Jesus on the cross. We have been given spiritual weapons through His Word!

God is present with us when we walk through pain and failure. I remember after first meeting my husband Dan, I felt a little uncertain about myself. The Lord was so gracious and merciful to me. I remember sitting in my car outside the office where I worked at the time and listening to a song on the radio. The words were so specific that I felt it was a special love song just for me from God. I remember calling the radio station to ask what the name of the song was, and as I shared a few of the words, they seemed to not have a clue about the song I heard on their station. You see, I wanted to buy the song so I could hear it again. I got out of my car and went back to work. It seemed to be specifically detailed for me! Later in my office at work, I sensed the Lord telling me to go to the Christian bookstore on my afternoon break.

After arriving at the bookstore, I remember being drawn by the Holy Spirit to a book on tape (at the time), *When God Whispers Your Name* by Max Lucado. I bought it and listened to it on the way home after work. Wow! I can remember it as if it were yesterday. The person reading the book was sharing how God spoke in an audible voice to this man through a mop bucket as he was cleaning a building. I knew, instantaneously, that my God, who holds everything in His hands, had spoken directly to me to encourage me! That is the love of the Father God! He let me know He was not caught by surprise by anything I had walked through and that He loved me so much He took the time to speak to me Himself! *God is speaking, and He wants us to recognize His voice.*

I remember on another occasion, as I was sitting in my car watching my son play softball and watching the soft raindrops hitting the windshield, I heard a specific, special word just for me as I was listening to Charles Stanley's message on the radio. I had been sick and was told to stay out of the damp weather. After hearing the message and listening for the order line, I ordered the tapes. When I received them, the special message I heard was not on the tape. The Lord whispered to my heart, "Don't waste your money on the tape because I am speaking to you personally." God speaks today. God was letting me know He had spoken to me, Himself, yet again! He knew I would be sitting in the car. He sent the rain to put me in a position to hear His Word. He goes out of His way to touch and encourage the brokenhearted. He goes out of His way to make sure we know we are secure in Him. He is reaching out to you today to let you know, my precious reading friend, just how special and valuable you are to Him as well. God has not changed! He is the same, yesterday, today, and forever. He still speaks. He speaks through His Word. He can speak to you through a total stranger. He is speaking to you through the words on the pages of this book.

CHAPTER 32

SPIRITUAL APPLICATION

Army of God

A spiritual application shows us a picture of the army of God. We must learn to submit to God's authority and understand the importance of God's Word. The secret to marriage is selflessness. An army operates as a team. It is not about my needs. It is about meeting the needs of my spouse. Our needs are met on the way to meeting the needs of our spouse.

In Song of Solomon 4:9–11 we see Solomon calls the woman his *sister* to emphasize their relationship as companions and his role as her protector. This does not suggest an incestuous relationship, although it may sound strange to modern-day ears. Ancient Near Eastern love poetry often uses the term or language of brother and sister to represent two people in love. He shares how he is captivated by one glance from her eyes and how he delights in her love. He calls his bride his treasure. He depicts her love as being far better than wine, comparing her as smooth, sweet, and sensuous. He lets us know he is totally in love.

In marriage, you must learn to talk about everything, your goals, your shared dreams and dislikes as well. She's not only his lover but also his best friend. Remember, men are visual and stimulated by sight. Solomon is moved by Shulamite's every action and captivated by her beauty. He knows to wait on God's perfect timing for everything that awaits him in his marriage to his soon-to-be bride.

God has proper timing in dating, courting, and engagement, and we must learn to wait for the right time to awaken love. Sex was created by God for our enjoyment in marriage. God encourages us to enjoy our sexual union to the fullest in marriage. There can be no guilt or shame in the deepest pleasure between a husband and his wife. We are to experience delight in intimacy.

Listen up, men! You must focus on spending time with your bride, talking with her, being tender with her, and giving non-sexual touches. Take time to listen to her without fixing the problem. When she wants to share something with you, it is not for your advice, but to listen to her from your heart. Women need affection. Open doors for her and take her hand, showing affection in public. Also, she needs to feel secure and at ease in your presence. She doesn't need the constant stress of not moving fast enough to meet your time schedule. This produces anxiety and fear in her life. She needs to know she is the most important person in your life and that she is number one above all others, including extended family and children.

Listen up, women! Your husband wants you to be his greatest cheerleader. A man thrives on his wife's approval and praise. A woman's words weigh far more than anyone else's words. Be his number one fan. See him as your champion. Defend him and never allow anyone to speak negatively about him in your presence. Be his companion or best friend. Last, but not least, learn to compliment or praise him. Find something to praise him about. He will rise to the level of your praise.

In scripture, we see that Solomon got home too late and she went to bed too early. They were experiencing bad timing. Can anyone relate? Timing in marriage is everything. You can do the right thing at the wrong time and it doesn't work. One little incident and people give up today. Solomon and his bride did not give up here. They learned resiliency in marriage. Shulamite knew how vitally important it was to connect with Solomon. She tells her girlfriends (daughters in Jerusalem) to tell him she is lovesick if they find Solomon.

We can experience rejection even in marriage. Shulamite has taken off her robe, and how can she put it on again after having washed her feet? It is evident Shulamite is upset with her husband and is not about to get out of bed and defile her feet. (See Song of Solomon 5:3.) Relationships are not always easy. Every marriage has bad timing, and disconnectedness, but seen in the context of the marriage that God puts together, all things work out. You might be thinking here, "Did I marry the right person?" If you are married, you are married to the right person. Don't allow the enemy to get you caught in the trap of reasoning! If you are experiencing trouble, find a trusted counselor.

What had Solomon done? Shulamite is upset at her husband and can't get over it. He has hurt her by coming home late, so she is going to hurt him by not unlocking the door. Does this sound familiar? Have you ever been upset at your spouse? The enemy sets us up to be upset! Don't throw in the towel. Learn to fight for your marriage! Two wrongs do not make a right.

Realizing our marriage is a training ground for our relationship with God, we would all live far more fulfilling lives by learning to live selflessly. We also see a type and shadow of Jesus coming back for us, His church. The military representation is likened to the body of Christ as a warrior. "Who is this that looks forth like the dawn, fair as the moon, clear and pure as the sun, and terrible as a bannered host?" (Song of Solomon 6:10, AMP). "Return, return, O Shulammite; return, return, that we may look upon you! [I replied] What is there for you to see in the [poor little] Shulammite? [And they answered] As upon a dance before two armies or a dance of Mahanaim" (Song of Solomon 6:13, AMP). In this verse Shulamite is a representation of the church. God is calling the church to repentance, to be fully restored and to arise. God's relationship with the church is a reflection of marriage. Marriage is a reflection of one's relationship with God. How you are treating your spouse is how you are treating God. Do you make time for your spouse and protect your marriage against attack?

God gives His army tremendous power and protection. "'No weapon formed against you shall prosper, and every tongue which rises against you in judgment You shall condemn. This is the heritage of the servants of the

LORD, And their righteousness is from Me,' says the LORD" (Isaiah 54:17, NKJV). (Also see Revelation 11:3–6 for further study.)

No matter what you have experienced or how many times, God's mercy and grace are still available to you; you are not alone! Learn to share your story. Rise up and be the Army of God. Share your story to turn others to Christ before the end of the age.

HOLINESS AND CHARACTER PROCESS

All of the real excellence and holiness on earth center in the church. Christ goes forth subduing his enemies, while his followers gain victories all over the world, the flesh, and the devil. We, as His followers, see the tenderness of a Redeemer, the delight He takes in His redeemed people, and the workings of grace in us. True believers alone can possess the beauty of holiness.

God reveals to us what is in our hearts through the things we walk through in life. How are you responding? What is in your heart? When someone fails, what are your first thoughts? Do you have a heart of compassion and mercy, or are you the first to jump on the bandwagon of gossip? Take a look at your thought life. Do you see the positive or negative? Ask God to purify your heart!

When our real character comes forth, as God works His will in our lives, we will be commended. Both the church and believers, at their first conversion, look forth as the morning, their light being small, but increasing. As to our sanctification, we, as believers, are represented as fair as the moon, deriving all our light, grace, and holiness from Christ; and as to our justification, clear as the sun, clothed with Christ, the Sun of righteousness, and fighting the good fight of faith, under the banners of Christ, against all spiritual enemies. (See Song of Solomon 6:4–10.)

YOUR STORY WILL BRING GOD GLORY

Sometimes we go through so many broken places in a short period of time that we begin to feel like we stay in the desert or wilderness. After my daddy's death, my mother's home was vandalized and robbed on April 1st of

2010 while we were on a trip. My mother and I started a mother/daughter trip after she retired. My sister and I loved going to the beach with Mom. After she changed careers and went into nursing, Mom and I continued our yearly trip during April. I remember making the reservations early that year in February, and a few days later, I sensed the Lord nudging me to leave a couple days sooner. I asked my husband if that was all right and called the resort to start our trip earlier. After arriving at the coast, I had an uneasy feeling in my spirit. The Lord kept me awake in the early morning hours praying, and He gave me Psalm 59 and a couple other verses about His divine protection. Two nights went by the same way. On April 1st, we went out to the pool after breakfast, and just before noon I sensed we should go in early and get an early dinner.

Mom agreed, so we went in to get dressed for the evening. No sooner than we arrived to do a little shopping and park the car, my mother's phone started ringing. She was scrambling to find her phone in her purse. She answered to find my sister in total hysteria and frantically yelling that Mom's home had been burglarized. They took all her jewelry, televisions, Daddy's guns, tools, ladies designer handbags, and everything else of value. They even took the box for the television that we had given Mother and Daddy for Christmas. My sister and cousins came over as well as the sheriff's department and a detective. I shared the scriptures with the detective and told him he should start praying the scripture on how God reveals all hidden truth to me and shows me things to come (John 16:13) because he needed that for his line of work.

The most amazing thing happened. Every time I would begin to think about the criminals vandalizing my parent's home and stealing all their possessions of value, it made me very angry. Immediately, I would pray the scriptures He gave me back to Him. God hears and answer our prayers. He gives us a *rhema* word for our specific circumstances. The scriptures God gave me were Psalm 59, Psalm 33:10, and John 16. We began to pray for the thieves that God would open their spiritual eyes, bring them to repentance and confession, and that they would be so miserable they would have to confess and turn themselves into the law; but also that they would receive Jesus as Lord and Savior.

We spoke with the detectives off and on over the next several weeks. In June, one of the detectives called us telling us he had good news and bad news. The bad news: the thieves had stolen everything and they had sold it on the black market. The good news: they had caught the robbers. The detective told us they hardly ever catch thieves that break in and steal from homes. I had assured him that based on the scriptures God gave us at the beach that God was going to bring them into derision, which is public humiliation. Exactly as God's Word said, that is what happened!

One of the other detectives on the force was watching a suspect, and after stopping him for questioning, he began taking something out of his pockets which was old money and throwing it in the backseat. The man told the detective he was so miserable he had to get it off his chest and rode around with him showing him all the homes they had robbed over the last two years. He showed the detective where my parents lived and told how they robbed her home as well. He said he sent his sister to the door with her cell phone. If someone came to the door, she would show them a picture of her dog on the phone and say she was looking for him. If no one came to the door, the two men in the car would break in and rob the home.

I give thanks to God that He spoke to my heart to go to the beach earlier or my mother would have been home during the robbery. She would not have gone to the door for a stranger. This meant they would have broken in on her while she was at home.

This is just another amazing example of how God spared and saved my mother from this tragic event. We learned later that the first name of one of the men was "Confessor." His mother had named him Confessor, and he had to confess. God is amazing and sometimes has a sense of humor too. We also learned this young man had been arrested as a juvenile for stabbing a classmate years before. God brought His Word to pass over my mother and this situation. The Word of God works when we pray it back to Him.

CHAPTER 33

SATAN'S ATTACK ON YOUR FAITH

Persevere Beyond Circumstances

Satan attacks your faith through circumstances. You can get a picture of going through many tough circumstances as you have read so far. When you and I get to the place where we feel overwhelmed by seemingly unbearable circumstances, we can reflect on the Psalmist David as he wrote, "My heart is severely pained within me, And the terrors of death have fallen upon me. Fearfulness and trembling have come upon me, And horror has overwhelmed me" (Psalm 55:4–5, NKJV).

When you search the scriptures for yourself, you will be amazed to find that David spoke more of trusting God than anyone in the Bible. He spoke more about seeking after God and waiting in His presence than any other writer. David found the secret of waiting upon the Lord for renewed strength in the time of greatest need. David was waiting on God while going about his daily duties while tending the sheep in the fields. God knew exactly where he was and what he was doing. David also told us he feared no evil, even though he walked through the valley of the shadow of death, because he had come to know the Lord in such a personal manner that he totally trusted God and knew He was with him. *God wants us all to get to this place!*

When we feel like we are walking through an attack of the enemy on all sides, we too, can come to the place where we say as David did, "All men are liars!" David obviously spoke out of his overwhelming pain, anguish, and sorrow, when he allowed this to come out of his mouth. Not forgetting that David was "a man after God's own heart," we can see how anyone could experience an attack against their individual faith in God and be shaken to the point of speaking negatively.

When we have prayed and cried out to God, yet do not understand why we stay in a situation of grief and despair, we are prone to wonder what is going on. David was at a place of despair as many of you are reading this now. David was not accusing God of lying, but I am sure he felt, as many of us have on occasion, total desperation with all the lies from the enemy. Have you ever felt like escaping or running away to another country to get away from the pain? Geography is not the problem. David cried out also, "...that I had the wings like a dove, I'd fly away from all this despairing and find a place of rest" (Psalm 55:6, AMP).

I understand seasons of pain and sorrow. After the loss of my daddy in January of last year, then the robbery of my mother's home in April, to someone very close to me walking through abandonment with two kids, to my pet of seventeen years having a stroke, and walking through betrayal with business partners in one company, life can get a bit overwhelming. When it seems like everywhere you turn things are happening like this, you are walking through a season of attack against your faith.

I will not be moved by what happens in this life, because I know my God is with me. He is with me and my husband, and He is for us. He is with our family and your family too! He has a great plan for us, and we have already won the victory through Christ Jesus! During these times of trials, we have to double-up on the Word of God and keep pouring in through listening to CDs and sermons, praying constantly, and surrounding ourselves with likeminded people.

I have been praying for my cat Cherub. I know if I don't have enough faith to believe for my pet, I had better not pray for any people I know that have need of healing. I have watched God through the process of healing him with his little back legs getting stronger each day. We have been giving him therapy as we bathe him each evening and carry him to and fro from the litter box. We had to watch him more closely all day. He was unable to walk and was going around in circles because he had lost the use of one leg almost totally. We can get that way too. It seems we are just circling rather than getting to the finish line. God is still faithful. Just like we carried Cherub to and fro to the litter box and held him each night, allowing him to lie on my chest close to my heart while we rested in the evenings, God holds us close to His heart too. He wants us to rest in Him and come to the place of healing. God brings healing and launches us into our destiny so we can finish well. We are here until it's time for us to go home to be with Him.

When we experience God's amazing love, we believe, trust in, and expect great things to happen because God loves us and He is a good God! When you feel like life is passing you by or you feel stuck circling in the desert, choose to climb up in the arms of your heavenly Father where you can hear the heartbeat of God and feel His amazing love. When we cling to God and renew our minds with the Word, we will be healed too!

"As for me, I will call upon God, And the LORD shall save me. Evening and morning and at noon, I will pray, and cry aloud, And He shall hear my voice. He has redeemed my soul in peace from the battle that was against me, For there were many against me" (Psalm 55:15–18, NKJV). Run to God and find a place to sit in His presence. Ask God for His peace. Pray the promises of God back to Him. God wants us to trust Him, rely upon Him, and expect Him to be faithful to His Word, for He is always faithful!

CHAPTER 34

EMOTIONAL DISTRESS

The Place of Choice, Focus, and Surrender

Emotional distress pulls us apart at the seams. The definition of stress goes far beyond the mental and emotional process that causes distress. It is important to recognize that mental processes have physical consequences as well. We must learn to part from the distractions and choose to spend time with God, or we will come apart.

Fear and anger are the two most common reactions to stress. Most psychologists teach that fear and anger are opposite sides of the same coin. What this means is that both emotions exist in a pair. Have you ever experienced anger and fear at the same time about the same situation? Fear is the process of worry or anticipating events that may never really happen. One may fear what could happen. We must remember "would have, should have, and could have" always comes from the enemy. He attacks our minds with this wrong way of thinking. It can become obsessive-compulsive. Anger is a possible response to pain or loss for ourselves or those we love. Anger can also be a clue that something is not quite right or a form of protection. Whether real or perceived possibilities, our bodies begin to respond to both while we are in this desert place.

For example, you might get worried about your health because of something you heard or what has happened to family members. Maybe you have already had cancer and the threat of having it again can produce stress if you dwell on it. Then you find a lump or little spot, or a new ache and pain, a change that is not anticipated that sends out a signal to your brain to think about it. This action sends out a signal to warn, which signals you to choose to obsess about if you are not trained how to use God's Word over your circumstances. His Word is truth and outweighs fact. We don't have to believe every report from the enemy. You can choose to worry or choose to trust God.

Let's just say for example, you have been in an automobile wreck where there was a fatality and you lived. When you are a passenger in a car with a bad driver, you will probably experience stress due to the trauma you experienced before. Some people respond with fear and others with anger due to the careless driving that places all in danger.

The stress response is basically the same whether the issue of concern is large or small. The stress response is also basically the same whether the concern is about ourselves or someone we care about. Our senses act as a transmitter sending information to us from outside or inside our bodies. Our five senses (sight, smell, sound, taste, touch) plus our own intuition help us to comprehend the unknown, and through our intellect we determine what we might experience. In our minds, we project what may or may not happen in the future and then assess whether we have the resources needed to deal with the issues at hand. If a person continually dwells on the circumstances and begins to worry, our body stays in a stressful state.

Stress is a survival mechanism. Stress also allows us to perceive and forecast what resources we may need with some type of accuracy. We perceive this through our intellect and experiences, whether bad or good. With too many difficulties or bad experiences, we have a tendency to think negatively, and we may think there is a dark cloud hanging over us. The enemy tries to get us to think negatively and predict bad outcomes. It is like an evil foreboding. Satan wants us to agree with his plan over our lives, which is defeat and destruction. God has a great plan for our lives, and He turns *all* things out for our good and His glory when we apply His Word to our lives and trust Him, even in the darkest times.

It is important to ascertain and learn the function of the human body and learn how we respond through our emotions. If I can get people to renew their minds, start reading the Word of God and praying daily, and deal with distractions ruthlessly, I can guarantee them they will soon see the well in the desert and learn to trust God daily as He provides and protects.

When a person has lived in survival mode for too long, he or she has a tendency to be a little harder to grasp the understanding than others. We must come alongside and share our own stories of God's intervention to give them hope. Some people get into pity parties and nobody shows up. Others will find an audience and tell everyone they meet, even total strangers, of the horrific events they have experienced. When a person has experienced many tragedies, they may initiate the "fight-or-flight" response, releasing copious amounts of adrenaline; or based on past failures to cope, an opposite response is learned helplessness and defensiveness, which releases immune-suppressing hormones and chemicals.

After you have experienced abuse, abandonment, divorce, or many other stressors such as frequent moves or loss of jobs, you are likely to not be able to see yourself up for any task, and will feel overwhelmed and desperate. On the other hand, imagine the owner of the company you work for puts you in charge of a huge project and you know you can do a superb job because it is your gifting. You welcome the challenge and feel excited about a new opportunity. If you have gone through life on survival mode for an extended period of time, everything becomes a chore and hard to complete. When you perceive a situation as stressful, key areas of your heart are naturally activated that trigger the release of stress hormones into your blood, as I earlier mentioned. Your body doesn't know the difference between happy stress and negative stress. Stress is different for everyone and really depends on the individual's ability to cope. Stressful situations, whether real or perceived, still activate key areas in your brain. When a person lives this way for an extended period of time or for many years, chronic stress can lead to a host of medical problems as well.

For example, if you have lived with a spouse with anger and rage, your body may still be used to their perceived response, even long after God has brought healing to your spouse. Because you may have experienced long-term explosions and never know how they will respond, your natural body still responds in stress. This can produce sickness. You must ask God to heal your entire body.

Your naturally healthy body then becomes less able to resist infection, and your immune system can become impaired. You are at increased risk for developing depression, heart disease, and stroke. In the desert, you must take care of yourself emotionally right away. You don't have to please everyone and try to be perfect. Many times people live in situations with abusers that are obsessive-compulsive and lead to anxiety, immune support problems, and exhaustion. Have you ever been around someone who you knew was monitoring your every move? This creates unbearable stress. You aren't able to relax. God did not create us to live under constant scrutiny.

You must seek out others to help you walk through this time in your life. If you don't have the loving support of others, some people tend to over-exercise or find support in overeating, while others go shopping. I know most ladies like to shop anyway. I remember an elderly lady telling me that after her husband died she went shopping everyday for more than two years. While others waste away from not being able to eat, some pick up bad habits such as alcohol or various others means of covering pain and coping, rather than coming to the place of healing in God.

Life is in the eye of the beholder. When we view any situation as an opportunity, not as a threat, this is a healthy alternative. View life as an opportunity for growth and potential. Learn to take deep breaths, long walks, and spend time in the Word of God.

When we learn to cast our cares upon the Lord, we can find peace even in the midst of the greatest storm. No one knows the pain or heartache anyone else is experiencing. Only if you have walked in their shoes will you truly know and understand. *All circumstances are different, but God is the answer.* If you are not the one walking through the desert, you must realize that when you encounter a friend or associate who is walking through extreme circumstances to ask God to give you His eyes to see with and His heart to feel what they are feeling. Since it is *only God* who can bring healing, you and I can rest in knowing the Holy Spirit will help us know how and what to do for those around us who are hurting.

When you walk through or live in extended periods of stress and negativity, it can change your outlook on life if you do not choose to stay focused. It is vitally important to always inquire of the Lord and keep Him as your number one guide for life. Let's look at Job's story.

JOB'S STORY

Job was considered by God to be the most upright and blameless man in all the earth. God showed Satan that there was a person on earth whose love and devotion to God could stand the test of trial and difficulties. Job had been blessed by God, and then God allowed Satan to take it all away. There are many theories about what, why, and how, but I believe Job had fear of what might happen, too, that opened the door for enemy access. God allowed Satan to afflict Job with physical pain and sores all over his body. Job shared his grief with his friends who listened patiently for days. Then, his friends decided to find answers for why and began to reason and justify. His friends sat and listened to Job. Job's wife told him to curse God and die.

Job asked God, "Why?" God reminded Job that He was still and always will be God. Job went through extreme, strenuous, heartbreaking trials of testing which we would consider going through hell on earth today. Through it all, Job learned a more valuable lesson, and that was learning to know God at a more intimate level. He also learned God's ways and understood God's character to a far greater depth, while developing a greater sense of awe and amazement in God!

Job knew God. He had not just heard about God, but he had a personal, intimate relationship with God! Many men and women have heard about God, heard other people's stories, but have not had their own personal experiences with God themselves. God wants us to experience Him! We each have a place of surrender.

DAWN'S STORY

It wasn't until Dawn's husband of twenty-one-plus years walked out on New Year's Eve that Dawn came to know the Lord in a greater and more personal way than ever before. It brought her to the place of being eternity minded, and she learned to trust God for her daily provision and protection. God amazed her with His love during this time. God always takes us through a place in the desert so we can help others walk through their own desert places as well. God does not waste your time in the desert. He uses what you have walked through to help others make it through. He shows Himself strong on your behalf so others will believe also.

Dawn learned and trusted God's ability to be her Husband after the husband of her youth abandoned her and the two children. When we share the depths of pain and heartache we have walked through, only then can others hear and understand the amazing healing power of God! We teach others to trust Him when we look back on how we trusted God in the desert and sleepless nights after betrayal.

Dawn was devastated and desperate. She desired just to hear her husband say he was sorry and wanted her back. He was no longer the same man she married. He had developed relationships outside the marriage, and wrong associations corrupt good manners. Dawn was in the darkest night of her soul, but she found the dawn appearing on the horizon when she learned to cast her care and trust in the Lord fully! *The more one has experienced in suffering, and sought God for healing, the more access and anointing there is to touch other people's hearts and the more doors God will open for you to help and encourage others.* He clears the path in the desert for you to walk in His streams of goodness and *living water* to help others!

ALICE'S STORY

Alice's Addiction to Her Man

Another place of surrender may be an addiction. Alice was in love with a man that did not exist anymore. We are not really sure he ever did. Her husband never stood up to the plate to help with the financial responsibilities and cared more about the horses in the field or his riding trips than he did taking care of his own family. Alice carried the weight for the family due to his lack of concern. He never contributed much to the marriage in the way of finances at all. Alice and her husband had a great sex life, but the rest was another story. Alice was used to him being there for thirty years and learned to put up with his casual affairs, drugs, alcohol, strip club adventures, and lack of financial responsibility because she was used to him being there. In some way, she had put him up on a pedestal, and when he left, she felt like the carpet of her life had been pulled out from under her. She had unknowingly allowed him to take the place of God in her life. She had become addicted to him sexually and did not know what a good relationship actually was until God opened her eyes to see the truth. When a couple really understands the covenant of marriage and submits to God, there is unconditional love exhibited, with an understanding they have made a commitment to each other and God for life.

Her husband's parents always bailed him out of everything and told him he could do no wrong. He grew up with no boundaries and actually felt shame hidden beneath the scars in his heart to feel adequate to others. He always felt he had to flirt with other women to feel good about who he was. He had made his way to the altar to accept Jesus as some point, but he never renewed his mind to the Word of God. Thus, his fleshly nature won the battle that raged most of the days of his life. He had turned his back not only on his family, but also on God.

Alice experienced great disappointment through his leaving and lack of concern. She had trouble comprehending how anyone could actually do this with a conscience. She felt she had never known him with his cursing like a sailor and hateful attitude and a heart full of bitterness. Once her husband had an affair with another woman, he became one with her also. His heart became hardened to the things of God. He had fragmented soul ties with many women; therefore, he was never happy with any woman. His bad choices brought devastation to Alice, their children, and to the rest of the extended family.

God brought Alice through to the side of healing in her entire life. Much pain and heartache with intensive counseling brought Alice to a place of wholeness. She finally realized who she was in Christ and that her self-worth was not based on her husband's actions. Alice told me the pain was overwhelming at times and the thought of her husband from her youth being with another woman was unbearable. She took him back once before after the last affair several years ago because her children begged her to forgive him and let him come back home. She tried to make the marriage work, but it was apparent he did not. God brought Alice to a place of decision where she realized she had to put a line in the sand after numerous affairs. She moved on and found healing in God, while her husband lives with regret.

SUZANNE'S STORY

Suzanne lived in a foreign nation and had a great career. She thought she fell in love with a man from America and followed him. She could not get her proper papers, so she crossed the desert with a girlfriend through Mexico on foot to seek after this man that promised her the world. When she arrived in the United States, she learned he was lying to her and already had a wife. She had broken the law and could not easily get back to her country. She would have died for this man. She and her friend were robbed on the way over of their jewelry and money. What is a girl to do when she follows her heart and finds herself at the end of the desert with no one she knows?

TAMMY'S DATE NIGHT

We must all plan a time with our Lord and lover, and spouse. *We focus on our relationship.* Tammy loved her husband dearly. He was a godly man with strong moral values. Her husband loved his job. He and Tammy had been married for thirty-one years before Jim began to drift away. Jim became so involved with his work that he began to notice he was developing interest in another. Tammy would set the table for romantic dinners while Jim sat across from her gazing into her eyes and holding her hands. Slowly, as the years progressed, he began to hold something else, his phone. Tammy jokingly told Jim she was only setting the table for two from now on. Before it was too late, Tammy was able to share with her precious husband that he seemed to have lost interest in spending time with her. He was more interested in spending time on the phone with others rather than focusing on his wife who was in his presence. Wow. Does this sound familiar? Jim was so disconnected from his wife that he drifted more toward his job and was placing his work and the people that might call above his relationship with his wife. Thank God it was not too late for this couple. Learn to be where you are and spend time talking to the person who is in your presence.

WHO IS STANDING IN YOUR PRESENCE?

I remember being on a flight from Irvine, California, about ten years ago and noticing the flight attendant was a very beautiful older woman. I sensed she was a little down in her spirit, so I began to talk with her as she served us on the plane. Earlier that morning the Lord had woken me up saying, "I wish my people wanted to spend as much time with me as they do talking to people on their cell phones." I noticed a gentleman who was sitting just in front of me still speaking to someone through his ear piece attached to his phone. When the flight attendant asked him if he would like something to drink, he totally ignored her. She asked him again, and I will never forget what he said, "Can't you see I'm on the phone lady?" was his rude reply. I motioned for her to come nearby so I could share what God had whispered to me that morning. I told her about what happened that morning and that I had noticed people are more interested in talking to others that are miles away rather than those standing in their presence.

When we get our focus adjusted, and we begin to think eternity minded, we too will be able to see through God's eyes. We will see our well in the desert. We will see the beauty of God's creation and the way He orchestrates our days to grasp our attention. His love far surpasses anything in this life. God cares about the details, and nothing is accidental or coincidental in life.

ORDERED BY GOD/WAITING

God sees everything. *There is nothing that God can't see!* I remember the phone call from the doctor's office telling me I had to have a stat CT scan. As I drove to the hospital, I trusted God for everything. I didn't really experience any fear because I know God is in control. Earlier in the week, apparently the lab had made an error and not ordered the blood work properly. When my doctor found out, she was very concerned and phoned me to tell me she woke up through the night thinking about me. She explained she wanted the test done to find out what was going on.

After the scan, I was asked by the technician to sit and wait in the patient lobby area for the results. We waited and chatted in the waiting room with the other people who seemed to be a little nervous. Then the technician walked over and handed me a phone with my doctor on the line. She said they accidentally found a problem and they would be scheduling more tests. I remember later that evening the Lord spoke to my heart to read Proverbs 16:33. After reading it and studying, I knew God was showing me He would take care of everything, not to worry, and that as I acknowledge Him in all my ways, He is watching over me. The next morning I felt led to read the same scripture in the amplified version of the Bible. The Bible says, "The lot is cast into the lap, but the decision is wholly of the Lord [even the events that seem accidental are really ordered by Him]."

God always sees everything! Even the lab department making an error was part of the plan. If they had not made the error, the stat CT scan would not have been ordered. God was making sure the truth was going to be revealed. Every step was ordered by God.

Have you ever known or sensed something was not quite right, even in your health? You perhaps have gone to many doctors who can't explain the problem and symptoms until one day they accidentally find the problem. God orders our steps, and He exposes all hidden truth so we can receive whatever we have need of at the time. God is amazing. He always knows just how to encourage us. That is the amazing love of our Father God! No matter what you might be going through, He is the well in the desert. He is the fountain that never runs dry. He is our very present help in time of trouble. He is the author and finisher of our faith. He is interceding for you right now, that your faith would not fail. He loves you with an everlasting love, and it is with His loving kindness that He draws us to Himself!

WAITING IN THE DESERT

Dawn found herself in the midst of a desert after her husband betrayed her. She experienced such excruciating pain in her heart that she would just sit and cry to the point of sheer desperation. One minute she was weeping, and the next minute she felt like taking matters into her own hands due to her husband's betrayal.

Parents of wayward children feel the pain as well. Parents who raise their children to know God can still have children who grow up and make really bad choices. When the enemy sets his traps to ensnare someone, he sends demonic forces in to destroy lives and entire families. Satan comes to steal, kill, and destroy. He blinds people to the truth so they begin to reason and start thinking wrong thoughts. Wrong thoughts turn into wrong actions, and can eventually lead to sin and destruction.

Perhaps you, too, are walking through your own health issue or relationship issue. You may be the parent of a wayward son or daughter. You may be the one who was left in the middle of the desert. Always remember that no matter how wonderful a parent you may have been, children can make wrong choices. Don't blame yourself. Keep praying and fasting for them. Pray for your spouse or for your children to come to their senses like the prodigal son. Commit them to God.

Perhaps you are the spouse that has been abandoned and feel all alone. You are most likely crying out to God for it to end. It is in the waiting where we are strengthened. In our weakness, God becomes our strength. He wants us to trust Him and lean on Him every minute of the day. When we walk through the desert, we learn to fully trust and depend on God at a new level. Our flesh is crucified by the things we walk through. The Bible says, "Every one that is proud in heart is an abomination to the Lord; though hand join in hand, he shall not be unpunished" (Proverbs 16:5). *God desires that we surrender our entire heart to Him.* God knows the little places of pride that are so easily erected in the heart. The places where you know you have ignored the warnings from God but have chosen to go your own way. When we choose to ignore the warnings of the precious Holy Spirit, our heart becomes hardened in areas. This is pride. When we surrender to God, we learn to hate evil, arrogance, pride, and perverted and twisted speech. (See Proverbs 8:13.)

The Bible says, "By mercy and truth iniquity is purged: and by the fear of the LORD men depart from evil" (Proverbs 16:6). God purges us in the desert. He takes everything out of us that is not like Him. Dying to self daily is accomplished when we choose to do the right thing, even when we feel like doing the wrong thing, because a little more of our flesh is crucified so we can become like Christ.

The Bible says, "When a man's ways please the LORD, he maketh even his enemies to be at peace with him" (Proverbs 16:7). It is in the desert where we learn to trust God, rely on Him totally, expect His provision and learn to apply the blood of Jesus to every area of our lives. Sometimes the best place to be is flat on your back. The only place left to look is up. God is there! He has always been there. He is waiting for you to respond to Him today. Whether you have worked in a strip club and lived like you were going to end up in hell to whether you are a minister who has lost his way, God is still waiting for you to see your well in the desert. Whether you are walking through divorce or being abandoned by your best friends and associates, God will never leave you nor forsake you.

The best place to be is on your knees in prayer. We learn the most in the school of *kneeology*. This is the place of prayer where we learn to ask God first and obey His every instruction. All of us have chosen to go our own way in some area and found ourselves in a desert. Remember, there is hope in God! We must learn to wait on God. We forfeit the miracles when we fail to wait on God. We miss our transformation and our testimony when we refuse to wait. We miss our intimacy with God. We miss faith when we run ahead of God. Be willing to wait on God and trust Him.

CHAPTER 35

CHILDREN WITH BROKEN HEARTS

Don't Forget the Children

Let's not forget the children that are left wounded and angry after the fallout of betrayal, separation, divorce, or abuse. They grow up angry and full of fear if not healed. Children need a father and a mother in the home. Their hearts are scarred from abandonment and divorce as well as the parents. They must confront and/or get counseling to start the process of healing.

God told us our problems in life come out of our own hearts. Adultery does not happen by accident. It starts in the heart and is allowed to develop until it totally contaminates the heart. When your heart is contaminated with wrong thinking, you do things that will embarrass and destroy you later in life. Have you ever wondered or said, "Why did I say or do that?" Apparently, it was in your heart.

Christian parents who abandon their child or children hate themselves for it, but the action was a result of contamination in their hearts. The Christian who takes a wrong path and ends up in sin is ashamed. Whatever is in your heart will eventually appear in your behavior. Children pay for the fallout with damaged emotions as well.

No two children respond the same way. Isn't it amazing that you can discipline one child when caught for lying and he is immediately sorry, asks for forgiveness, and feels really bad about it, while the other one is angry, bitter, and distances himself from all authority figures and the ones that love him? Your attitude determines whether your heart softens or hardens in the presence of God's truth. God will send a prophet to shine the light on the darkness to expose the enemy. He does this because He loves us.

The light of God's Word that softens one's heart can also have a hardening effect on another person in the same room. Sometimes people develop a hard heart due to what they have experienced. Feeling like you have to be tough or hard due to tough roads in life can damage the soul. However, a hard heart does not make you stronger or tougher. It just breaks more easily than a soft heart. Teenagers act out their hurt in anger. Hurting people hurts others. They look for ways to cover their pain. God wants to heal our children's hearts and ours too.

God wants us to have soft, tender, pliable hearts that are moved with compassion and repentance at the slightest thought of sin. While some people have pure hearts and a strong desire to please God, others have developed a hard shell to cover pain and enable them to weather the desert storms in life. You can wonder if children actually came from the same set of parents due to their differences.

If a child exhibits a problem of submitting to God, to people, and to those in authority, it is an immediate sign that you are dealing with a hard heart. Teenagers aren't the only ones who have submission problems when it comes to authority. They are normally imitating what they have seen in their home. *Can you submit?*

If you make excuses for bad behavior instead of taking responsibility for your own actions, you have a problem with authority and have a hard heart. James 4:6–8 says, "He gives more grace...'God resists the proud, but gives grace to the humble.' Therefore submit to God. Resist the devil and he will flee from you. Draw near to God and He will draw near to you. Cleanse your hands, you sinners; and purify your hearts, you double-minded."

You are unable to focus on God when you are double-minded. Learn to trust God and open your heart to submit to God-given authority that He has placed in position for your protection. Submission is absolute evidence of a focused heart. If you are resisting and becoming defensive, don't underestimate the power of the enemy at work in hardening your heart toward the things of God. Watch for these signs in your children. Don't tolerate bad behavior. Help them walk through their desert too.

Children with emotional problems grow up to be adults who are overly sensitive and sometimes hear things incorrectly. They live their life in drama, always thinking someone doesn't like them. In other cases, you will recognize someone with a damaged heart because it is a strained relationship. It is almost as if you have to walk on egg shells to keep peace. The spirit of rejection sets them up to be upset.

Do your children have a desire to learn? Do you, as a parent, have a desire to learn? The Bible says, "LORD, You have heard the desire of the humble; You will strengthen their heart; You will incline Your ear" (Psalm 10:17, NASB). When you have a teachable spirit, a hunger for the things of God, and are meek in your attitude, these are clear signs of a desire to learn. If you allow your children to get away with not helping in the house, not learning responsibility, and ignoring bad behavior, you are raising a child whose life will be a wreck. Have you ever encountered a teenager that knew everything? It is amazing how smart they begin to realize their parents are when they get a little older.

Even during difficult storms in life, you must not ignore your children's needs when feeling like you are barely making it yourself. If you do, you will have children that grow up to repeat the cycles of sin they have witnessed. Be honest with your children and take time to help them through the desert they have been placed in due to sin. Seek godly counseling for them and keep the lines of communication open.

Jesus said, "...unless you are converted and become like children, you will not enter the kingdom of heaven" (Matthew 18:3, NASB). We must not ignore the fact that teenagers have to learn to deal with hurt and anger when going through a storm as well. No matter what age your child or children in the home, God has blessed you with them to train and nurture in the things of God. When you find yourself in a desert with brokenhearted children, don't throw in the towel, but turn to God for His wisdom. One of the greatest attributes of a child is his curiosity and desire for knowledge. Children are not stupid, and they understand far more than you think they do. Remember, a sign of a soft heart is a teachable spirit or willingness to learn and a hunger for the things of God. *Do you have a teachable spirit? Do your children?*

Be open and honest with your children. The entire family experiences pain, anger, and hurt when facing a desert of divorce and betrayal. One minute you might be fine and the next you are a wreck. Surround yourself with godly counsel and stay in church. Don't isolate yourself from others. Don't allow your children to isolate themselves from church and family. "A man who isolates himself seeks his own desire; he rages against all wise judgment. A fool has no delight in understanding, but in expressing his own heart" (Proverbs 18:1–2).

Don't forget that discipline is a part of love. We must stop making excuses and take time for our children. When people find themselves in a bad situation, it is usually due to a lack of discipline. Teach your children the small things in life and build discipline and self-control into the treasure of your child's heart and your own. Don't make excuses!

When adultery occurs it is grounds for divorce and grounds for forgiveness. God forgives when we truly repent. However, there are consequences in the natural that are long lasting. It can take years to rebuild trust, not only with your spouse, but with the children as well. Adultery can leave your children and you with abandonment and rejection issues. Adultery destroys your relationship with your spouse, your children, and is sin against God. If you are in the middle of a separation, I urge you to seek counsel for godly wisdom. If you both are willing to stay and pray and believe God for reconciliation, there is hope for the marriage and family. True repentance is necessary. When one truly experiences brokenness and godly sorrow, nothing is impossible with God. God is the great reconciler. With God, all things are possible.

A young man I know, who experienced abandonment, wrote this poem for a class assignment about what he wanted most in life.

ALL I WANT

All I want is someone who won't walk out on me,
Someone to treat me like a son.

All I want is someone who won't walk out on me,
Someone to care about me.
Someone to talk about sports.
All I want is someone who won't walk out on me,
Someone to love me.
Someone to talk to when I am down.
Someone who will do stuff with me.
Someone who will understand me.
All is want is a dad who loves me.

—T. LOGAN, used by permission

As I read this poem for the first time, tears began to fill my eyes. There are hundreds of thousands of children that feel the same as this precious young boy. If you are a man who has abandoned your family or perhaps thinking about doing so, run to Father God for His help. If you are a mother who has abandoned her family, repent and turn back to God. He is waiting with arms open wide.

CHAPTER 36

TACTICS OF THE ENEMY

No Repentance

JACOB'S BROKEN SPIRIT

Jacob had everything going for him. He had a beautiful wife and family. He had a beautiful home and people that loved him. Jacob began to slowly develop relationships with bad associations that led him down a path of wrong choices. He had affairs and starting going to strip clubs for attention. His wife grew angrier and more hurt after every bad encounter. His wife, Sharon, kept waiting for his apology, but it seemed he was only sorry he had gotten caught; the real brokenness never came. He would sit and cry in his favorite chair but never moved to help his wife regain trust in him. He never stopped the affairs. His wife developed a root of bitterness and the cycle began. Because Jacob never repented and never started in the process of healing to bring wholeness to his marriage, Sharon had a deepseated fear of him having an affair again. Jacob did not take the time to make sure Sharon knew she was number one in his life.

Jacob grew weary of the tongue lashings and just gave up. His spirit became broken, and he felt like all he wanted to do was escape. *Jacob had a broken spirit.* If he had only repented and sought counseling, their marriage could have been saved. When two people are not working at the same time, the cycle begins. I call it "chasing the dog's tail" as that is how it would appear. One day the husband wants to work on the marriage and the wife is angry. Then when the wife is hurting and needs reassurance to walk through healing, the enemy has set a trap of a harlot in the street to seduce him into sin. The devil's plan is always destruction. (Read Proverbs 5–7.)

If couples would only learn to apply the blood of Jesus to their minds, marriage, and money, they could succeed! The blood of Jesus is our place of refuge. It is a fortified place where the enemy is unable to penetrate. By faith, we apply the blood of Jesus by saying so out of our mouths out loud.

DEANNA'S DATE RAPE

Deanna came home from work early one day and caught her husband with another woman, her best friend. After the divorce, she had just started to date when this new man in town noticed her. She decided to go out with him and found herself on a dark road in the midst of her worst nightmare. She experienced date rape and was thrown from the car, leaving her in a desert with shame, regret, and fear of telling the authorities. Has this happened to you?

There is healing in Jesus Christ. He is our healer. He is the Great Physician. Our emotions need healing after such an experience, as well as the mind.

LYNNE'S GUILT

I remember sitting in front of a lady many years ago while she was doing my nails. She began to cry and shared a dream she had the night before with me. She said she saw this little boy running through this meadow filled with the most beautiful array of flowers she had ever seen. As she wept, the Holy Spirit spoke to my heart to ask her if she had ever had an abortion. I sensed it my spirit that God was showing her a son that had gone on before her. She admitted she had an abortion and was carrying guilt. I explained God's forgiveness when we come to Him. God gave me the gift of praying with her that day as she released the guilt and condemnation to the Lord and received His forgiveness. You see, I learned that the instrument they used was somewhat like a vacuum when she had her abortion. The vacuum that sucked the child out to his death also left a devastating vacuum to her soul. Only God can heal the heart and replace the vacuum or void that was left with His amazing love, mercy, and grace.

You may be reading this today, and just perhaps you have walked down the same path. There is forgiveness through the Son of God. Cry out to Him now and allow Him to remove the guilt, shame, and condemnation that come from the enemy when we carry sin and wrong choices. He loves you and wants to heal you! Not only is it important to receive God's forgiveness, but it is vital to forgive yourself. Sometimes what one needs is simply someone to take the time to care and listen. Women need their husbands to take the time to walk through the pain to healing with them. When a man says things like, "Just get over it" or "Are you going to bring that up again?" they probably don't realize the power of destruction through their words, or lack of concern.

SAM'S SHAME

Sam lived in shame and tried to hide his affairs. He was a little bit of a flirt all through school, and most came to know him as dangerous to be around. He casually would say things that were not quite appropriate, but everyone seemed to like him. Sam had a problem with drugs early on in his life but never truly got delivered. He hid the drug problem and tried other ways to cover his pain. He had so many affairs on his wife that he was afraid she would find out, so he figured he may as well play the field because she would find out one day anyway. He lived in fear of being found out. Sam wasted his baseball scholarship to have fun with the boys after graduation. He gave up on his dream.

Sam worked for a man who paid his salary under the table and never paid social security or taxes. Years later when a family wanted to help him get his contractor's license, he was unable to qualify as he did not have the recorded hours necessary since they were never turned in at all. Sam seemed to end up on the short end of the stick. Sam chose to take short cuts rather than working and maintaining anything. He would borrow another friend's equipment and just didn't seem to have the common sense to take care of what he had borrowed.

As a result of all Sam's bad choices, he lost his wife, family, job, and respect of friends. Sam never could seem to keep on the straight and narrow. He left home at an early age, and it seemed he could do no wrong. No matter what he did, his mother always came to his rescue. Sometimes it is hard to use tough love. As a result, Sam never left home emotionally or financially. He sought women to take care of him rather than stepping up to the plate to be a man. The end result was destruction.

We all know people like this or perhaps remember someone from college. It is sad when you know someone with so much potential and you wonder why they don't seem to observe the warnings from God or all the chances to repent. God loves everyone and desires that they come to know him. We must continue to pray for those we know who are lost. Pray that God opens their eyes to see Him and accept Him as Lord. One word from God can change a life.

TRIALS FOR TRANSFORMATION AND PURPOSE

Trials are where we are transformed and find our purpose. Most people come into alignment with Jesus, the Loving Savior, and learn about righteousness on an individual basis when facing a trial. When we walk through trials in the desert of life, we are transformed into His image when we submit, surrender, and say what He says about us. He is our righteousness, and we have individual testimonies of God's glory that align others to the Loving Savior Jesus Christ.

Trials teach us that God loves us and accepts us. They also teach of us of God's joy because of who He is. They teach us to trust Him because He is worthy! Trials transform our character and teach us to be eternity minded for the rest of our lives. God promises in His Word that He causes all things to work together for good to those that love Him (Romans 8:28). We learn how to help others once we have walked through trials of pain and suffering. We learn to comfort and minister to others. We learn that life is all about Jesus! It's all about you and me being transformed into His likeness. Trials are designed to make us like Jesus. How we respond during trials will reflect where we are with Christ in our daily walk.

CHAPTER 37

THE TAPESTRY OF LIFE

The Imperfections Turn to Perfection

We are like a beautiful tapestry that God weaves out of the threads of our lives. The back of any tapestry has imperfections and knots where broken threads are tied together. This is a little like life. We all have experienced broken places and things we might rather not share and times we have experienced pain and great suffering. You are God's masterpiece! He is carefully watching over your life.

FATHER IMAGE

Let's take a look at your upbringing for a moment. Some of you reading this still have hidden issues that relate to your father. Some are hurting and angry now just at the thought as you read this paragraph. We must take our memories to God and ask Him to heal our minds. There is no condemnation or guilt in the process of giving our past to the Lord so that we can move forward in a place of health and freedom. If the Holy Spirit brings things up that you have carried in your heart, ask the Lord to empower you to forgive and focus on your future and God's plan for your life. Don't sacrifice your future based on what has happened to you in the past (Mark 11:24–25; Philippians 3:13–14).

Since your heart is formed in the early years of life, it takes a healthy heart to grow and lead a successful life (Proverbs 13:12; 14:30, 33; 15:13; 17:22).

If you have forgiven your father and are on course producing the life you truly desire, small changes here and there will keep you growing. If you are not happy and have a nagging awareness that something still resides somewhere in your heart and you know it, then it will take drastic changes to create a new treasure in your heart (Matthew 12:35). You are a product of your environment and the things you have experienced. Change must occur to produce better habits. If you grew up without a Christian father, this lack can produce feelings of inadequacy, inferiority, insecurity, and defensiveness, which makes it difficult to grow and have good success in life. The feeling of being wanted and feeling valuable are essential to good mental health. It is a product of good parenting. Conviction is formed in a child with proper parenting as well. Giving your child choices with safe consequences when they are little helps build a sense of character and integrity with conviction for what is morally wrong.

When a child experiences abandonment by their father at a young age, it may create difficulty for the child to become strong and secure within themselves. Many get caught in the trap of becoming overachievers, while others can live in despair thinking they are unworthy of success; especially, if their parents told them they would never amount to anything or told them they were the black sheep of the family. This creates a fear of failure that causes some people to never do anything with their life. They just sit on the sidelines and watch their life coast along with no real drive for achievement or success. Since *fear opens the door to the enemy,* the secret things you fear can cause you to sabotage your own future and success.

With God, all things are possible. There is healing at the cross of Jesus Christ. There is healing when we bring our pain to Him. You might be asking me now, "How do I get healed?" If you are not in a church, find a Bible-based church that teaches the whole counsel of God's Word. Start reading the Bible and find a Christian counselor or trusted friend who can lead you to someone who can walk with you through the healing process. *Change comes through renewing your mind to the Word of God.* No Word, no change. Once you are born again or have accepted Jesus as Savior, you must read your Bible. Reading your Bible deposits the Word of God in your heart. Read Christian books about the father heart of God.

Renewing your mind to the Word of God will enable you to walk in the Spirit of God rather than in your fleshly nature. Read the Bible and listen to sermons while driving in your car. Get connected in church. A carnal Christian is one who accepted Jesus but failed to renew his or her mind.

Renewing the mind is a daily discipline of reading and praying God's Word. Ask God to give you His eyes to see with and His heart to feel with as you walk through this process. God will open your eyes to see and understand why your father may be the way he is at present. Understanding what he walked through will equip you to walk in forgiveness as well.

Remembering that the enemy blinds us to sin will enable you to walk in forgiveness. As you pray for those who have harmed you, God will produce His love in your heart. When you choose to pray for those who have brought you pain and heartache, you will realize the hate has been replaced with the love of God that only He can provide.

Many times, women or men who have had absentee fathers or did not understand the love of a father live searching for love in all the wrong places. They sometimes develop promiscuous lifestyles and become desperate as well. The enemy does whatever it takes to set us up for destruction. He comes to steal, kill, and destroy. God loves us and wants us to run to Him for our worth and value!

DESPERATE DORIS

Doris was desperate to get out of the house she lived in with her screaming parents. Her father had a temper, and her mother would sit and cry for hours. Doris could do nothing right in the eyes of her father. He seemed to be a drill sergeant and would criticize her constantly. Doris married the first man that came along and showed an interest in her. That marriage lasted almost two years and ended in divorce. The man she married turned out to be an adulterer with a hot temper like her father.

Doris was desperate to have a man in her life, so she moved to another city to find a better job. She climbed the ladder of success in the corporate world and married the first CEO that took her to dinner. He was fifteen years older and looking for a "trophy" wife. Doris stayed married to him for less than a year. He was controlling, domineering, and had obsessive-compulsive tendencies that left Doris a nervous wreck beyond all description. She could not focus at her job, so she had to resign.

Doris moved back to her home town to find a city filled with people who looked down on her in shame and disgrace. It was a small town with a religious mindset. The people thought divorce was the unpardonable sin. Little did anyone know, Doris had become so desperate she did not want to live and attempted suicide.

Doris was found by friends and taken to the emergency room where she was saved. After numerous failed relationships and two marriages ending in divorce, Doris turned to God and a local pastor and his wife for help. She sought God with her whole heart and found healing for her damaged emotions through the next two years. She ended up marrying a minister, and they travel the globe doing evangelism today. Doris did not allow the enemy to destroy her life. God still had a great plan for her. Doris did her part by seeking God and renewing her mind. Doris leads a women's ministry today and has three children that serve the Lord as well.

What the enemy means for harm to keep us out of God's perfect will, God will turn for our good and use for His glory! Give God glory by telling your story.

ABANDONMENT AND REJECTION

Annabelle felt betrayed. Her mother left when she was small, and she lived primarily with her father. She wanted a strong man with a great job. Annabelle married the first man that asked her who was becoming a doctor. He had a hot temper and did not really know how to communicate properly. He yelled at the kids, and they could not do anything right enough to please him.

After many years of marriage and devotion of her life to the kids while her husband, Richard, traveled, she found herself feeling the same abandonment issues and rejection when Richard came home and told her he was leaving. She was traumatized and devastated, begging Richard to stay. She began to smother him to the point of no return. Richard was much like his father who had affairs on his mother and deserted the family. Now Richard found himself walking in his father's shoes.

Because Annabelle's primary role model was her father, since he raised her, she looked to her father rather than to her husband for many years. This made Richard feel like "second fiddle" or "chopped liver" where he could never measure up to the image of Annabelle's father. When a husband and wife do not properly leave and cleave, marriage is extremely difficult, if not almost impossible. The Bible tells us we are to leave our parents and cleave to our spouse. This is the process of becoming one. "Therefore shall a man leave his father and his mother, and shall cleave unto his wife; and they shall be one flesh" (Genesis 2:24, KJV). Many couples do not fully understand the ramifications of God's boundaries and principles in His Word when not applied and adhered to as they are for our protection.

When a wife makes her husband feel less than number one, the enemy knows exactly how to set a trap to send someone by to make him feel affirmation and self-worth. Since men need respect, wives, you must choose to honor and respect your husband as unto the Lord. Do it, even when you don't feel like it, and sooner or later your emotions will line up with your actions. Begin to pray and ask God to change you so you can be the wife your husband so desperately needs!

Don't say everything that comes to mind. If you have to, stick your tongue out and bite down on it instead of saying wrong things. Whatever we sow is what we reap. What we say is how we open the door to the enemy for legal access to bring destruction. When we choose to say what God says about us and speak His promises over our lives and family, we are in line to receive good things from God Himself.

You choose daily by the words of your own mouth what your tomorrow will be like. *Do you really want everything that you are saying out of your mouth to come to pass?* Learn to see the well in the desert and every desert place as an opportunity for expedient growth to become more like Jesus.

DESIGNER BAGGAGE

I remember a few years back Spirit Airlines announced they would be charging for extra baggage when traveling. Then the other airlines started following suit. Since God has taught me there is always a natural manifestation to what is going on in the spirit realm, I have learned to pay attention in the natural. I remember sharing with my husband that God is showing America the high cost of having extra baggage and not dealing with the places in our lives that God has instructed us to deal with. When we choose to ignore the warnings from God, we pay a high price in life. When we choose to keep walking around the same old mountains of defeat and wind up in the desert again, we are acting just like the children of Israel who wandered forty years on what should have taken only eleven days. Can you imagine?

It is time we started looking in the mirror of God's Word and dealing ruthlessly with the sin that so easily besets us in our own personal lives. We all have something God is working on. No matter your worldly status or what you might have achieved in this life, God is not finished with you yet. It is when we choose to look in our own baggage and empty ourselves from our past that we can truly move forward with God. *When we stop running we will move forward.* When we stop running from God and covering our pain with designer baggage, we will receive God's healing. Your designer baggage may be your ministry that you have focused on over God and your family to the shame you still carry around from failed relationships. Your designer baggage may be your latest new home that you love more than God or even a special car, to your personal wealth in your bank account that you trust in more than God Himself. None of these things really matter when we become eternity minded. Look to Jesus! He is our very present help in time of trouble. When we choose to stop dragging designer baggage around with us and lay it all at the feet of Jesus, we will find perfect peace and healing through the blood of the Lamb of God, Jesus! Ask God to teach you how to seek Him first above all else.

SEEK GOD

Perhaps you have found yourself in one or more pages of this book and need help from God yourself. Whatever the case, inspire others to seek God first in their lives. Seek God as a Precious Jewel, Jesus, for He is the Lamb of God! Worthy is His Name! Jesus took your sin on the cross. He is your all in all. Come to Him and allow Him to pick you up and bring healing to your precious life. He has a great plan for you, and your life is not over! Jesus loves you so much and desires that you come to know Him at a higher level, a more intimate level, than ever before. Allow Him to be the treasure that you seek. Seek Him as a precious jewel. Never give up.

God gave His Only Begotten Son, the ultimate sacrifice, for you and me. Don't waste any more time in the desert. Embrace your pain and don't waste one more minute rehearsing the pain of the past. Choose this day to turn the pain and heartache into a story for God's glory. There are men and women who need to hear your story of how God brought you through the desert. Never give up on God!

CHAPTER 38

GOD RAISES US UP FROM THE ASHES

He Gives Us Beauty

God will raise you up out of the desert places and give you a brand new start. He takes great delight in healing us. He goes out of His way to make sure we find our way to Him and receive His healing that is so readily available. I am presently mentoring a young woman who is in extreme pain due to betrayal from her husband. The Lord gave me a dream and showed me a white door with me standing in front of it with the Lord. I saw this woman running to and fro between other doors. I knew God was standing beside me as well. God spoke to my heart to tell her, "When you stop running, you will move forward to healing."

She phoned me later in the day to tell me she knew what the dream meant now. God showed her she was praying one way one minute, and a totally different way the next. She was not getting into agreement with God for His plans in her precious life. She was hiding behind each doorway of pain. One was verbal and emotional abuse. Other doors were fear, abandonment, rejection, and betrayal. She realized she was in deep bondage due to all the extreme hurt and pain that she was hiding behind. It was not until God began to walk with her through all these doors that she began to heal, and it was extremely painful.

When you walk through a door, you must choose to come back through it to get to the other side. In order to receive healing from God, He must lead us to face hidden issues, people that have harmed us, truth that we find extremely difficult, and to face ourselves. We must not choose to bury our heads in the sand when we are in the desert because then our behind is still sticking up in the air. We must pull ourselves up and choose to move forward with God through to the place of wholeness and healing.

Many times people want to revert back to old ways of dealing with life rather than moving forward through the pain to reach the place of healing on the other side. A great scripture to memorize for these unbearable times of anguish is 1 Corinthians 10:13 where the Apostle Paul reminds us: "No temptation (no trial regarded as enticing to sin), [no matter how it comes or where it leads] has overtaken you and laid hold on you that is not common to man [that is, no temptation or trial has come to you that is beyond human resistance and that is not adjusted and adapted and belonging to human experience, and such as man can bear]. But God is faithful [to His Word and to His compassionate nature], and He [can be trusted] not to let you be tempted and tried and assayed beyond your ability and strength of resistance and power to endure, but with the temptation He will [always] also provide the way out (the means of escape to a landing place), that you may be capable and strong and powerful to bear up under it patiently" (1 Corinthians 10:13, AMP).

We are not always immediately delivered from pain and distress at the precise moment we cry out to the Lord. What we learn when going through seasons of pain is to trust in God and learn not to reason. Most people have a tendency to reason, just as it happened in the Garden of Eden. Reasoning produces confusion, which is never from God. We learn to trust that God is never wrong and that He is always with us. You and I may not understand what we are going through, but soon realize that in order to have a testimony one must walk through some seasons of opposition or pain. We overcome by the blood of the Lamb, and by the word of our testimony. (See Revelation 12:11.) It can be extremely painful when walking through a season of anguish and heartache. It also shows us what is in ourselves when we are tested and tempted. The most glorious part comes when we have reached the other side to healing and have overcome. We have a testimony to the greatness of God and His faithfulness.

When emotional pain is great, you can grow weary in waiting. You learn to confront the primary cause of pain when walking through to healing. The Holy Spirit will lead you through your time of pain in what and how to do it. It takes time. It is not an instant fix. Healing of the emotions is a process. God will bring you through the doors to the door of healing so that you will be able to step out again, even knowing the risk of getting hurt again. You learn to trust God above your circumstances. Remember that pain is a part of the healing process. Pain positions you to be in need of God. Stop fighting the pain and allow it to do its work. Don't waste the pain. Don't run from the pain. Endurance produces joy. "They who sow in tears shall reap in joy" (Psalm 126:5).

Ask God for help to endure to the place of healing. There is joy on the other side! Obey God quickly each time He whispers something to your heart and follow the leading of the Holy Spirit being fully assured that "weeping may endure for a night, but joy comes in the morning" (Psalm 30:5). Allow your pain to lead you out of bondage so God may form you into a priceless treasure to be used in helping others to the place of healing.

CHAPTER 39

MINISTRY OF HEALING

Begins on the Inside

The ministry of healing brings intimacy and trust. This is where we are amazed by God's love and seek Him above all else. The body of Christ rises up to bring healing to others. The Bible says, "Learn to do well; seek judgment, relieve the oppressed, judge the fatherless, plead for the widow" (Isaiah 1:17); "Pure religion and undefiled before God and the Father is this, to visit the fatherless and widows in their affliction, and to keep himself unspotted from the world" (James 1:27).

Today, more than ever, the church needs to rediscover its ministry to divorcees, singles, and surviving parents as the church is full of hurting people with a vast array of problems. The church is like a hospital for healing, not a cemetery to bury them. Let's take a look at the protection of God's law. "Ye shall not afflict any widow, or fatherless child" (Exodus 22:22). A widow can actually be a person who has an absentee husband or a husband who abandoned her. It places the woman in the same position. "Thou shalt not pervert the judgment of the stranger, nor of the fatherless; nor take a widow's raiment to pledge" (Deuteronomy 24:17).

"Remove not the old landmark; and enter not into the fields of the fatherless" (Proverbs 23:10). Prophets of old made it evident that men were not to fail to protect the widow and the fatherless (Isaiah 1:17;

58:6–10; Jeremiah 22:3). The Lord made specific practical provisions as we read, "And the Levite, (because he hath no part nor inheritance with thee,) and the stranger, and the fatherless, and the widow, which are within thy gates, shall come, and shall eat and be satisfied; that the LORD thy God may bless thee in all the work of thine hand which thou doest" (Deuteronomy 14:29). "When thou hast made an end of tithing all the tithes of thine increase the third year, which is the year of tithing, and hast given it unto the Levite, the stranger, the fatherless, and the widow, that they may eat within thy gates, and be filled...according to all thy commandments which that hast commanded me..." (Deuteronomy 26:12–13). Provision for widows and the fatherless was not from the king's treasury but from the Lord's house! "Bring ye all the tithes into the storehouse, that there may be meat in mine house..." (Malachi 3:10). If all God's people were obedient in giving, serving God instead of the world and materialism, there would be an abundance of meat in God's house to provide for the care of widows and the fatherless! The Lord also provided for the guidance, care, and counsel of widows. During this time and culture, when a husband died, the law stated his brother or next of kin must marry his widow.

This is where we find a perfect picture with Ruth when she came to the threshing floor *by night* and Boaz commanded that no one let it be known (Ruth 3:14). They did nothing wrong. Ruth simply had chosen Boaz, and Boaz desired her for his wife. The next of kin would have been Elimelech who had the first right of marriage. Perhaps, if Elimelech had known their desire to be married, he possibly could have resorted to extortion to obtain money from Boaz rather than taking off his sandal to indicate rejection (See Ruth 4:8). Perhaps this is why the secrecy. When polygamy was stopped, it still remained the next of kin's responsibility to counsel and watch over the widow and children.

Divorce is a far greater pain than death. It starts the cycle of carrying around morbid grief, without knowing how to process the pain, and it has a tendency to damage emotions and create issues with abandonment, rejection, and feeling ugly, unwanted, and a burden to others. There is massive "false" guilt that the enemy attempts to dump on divorcees. It also instills fear of the future and worry about how to make it financially. Women have a tendency to stop eating as a manifestation of covering pain and may lose extreme amounts of weight when dealing with abandonment and betrayal. Others may try to cover pain by overeating. When the pain becomes so severe that it may seem you are unable to endure, remember Hebrews 12:2 (AMP): "Looking away [from all that will distract] to Jesus, Who is the Leader and the Source of our faith [giving the first incentive for our belief] and is also its Finisher [bringing it to maturity and perfection]. He, for the joy [of obtaining the prize] that was set before Him, endured the cross, despising and ignoring the shame, and is now seated at the right hand of the throne of God."

INTIMACY AND TRUST

Intimacy is often difficult for someone who has walked through the desert of abusive relationships. Since *intimacy requires trust,* it must be restored before even the thought of intimacy is possible and comfortable for the abused. Abuse can create such a lack of intimacy that sex is not actually enjoyed in the holy covenant of marriage. When women have lived with angry men with outbursts of rage, it makes it extremely difficult to believe they will ever respond normally. Women can become so fearful of being hurt again, abandoned, and discarded that they find it virtually impossible to relax. Women can actually punish a good husband when they have fear of being harmed again. You must learn to trust God, not man. You will find it's much easier to trust God than man.

Choose to commit to do whatever God tells you to do to move to the place of healing. When a woman has been sexually abused or misused, she will have natural desires for her husband, but will not act on the desire to approach him. This can create damage to a godly husband. Trust the only living God and take obedient action to break free from the bondage.

When the Holy Spirit prompts you to do something, he is doing it to help you come out of your desert from desertion, abuse, mistrust, and abandonment. He is leading you out of the pain and into the oasis of God's plan for enjoyment of sex in marriage. People will oftentimes hurt you, but

God won't. God may lead you to a place that feels like hurt for a season, but God always works everything out for our ultimate good and His glory.

Learn to choose to do whatever God is showing you to do. Choose to refuse to live the rest of your life in the desert of fear and suspicion. People may have hurt you in the past, but don't allow them to destroy your future. Move forward in freedom! It may feel like getting out of quicksand, but God will be there to pull you out and lead you to His everlasting well in whatever desert you find yourself. Trust Him and renew your mind in the Word of God daily.

OVERCOMING FEAR AND HAVING A SOUND MIND

In 2 Timothy 1:7, the Word of God says, "For God hath not given us the spirit of fear; but of power, and of love, and of a sound mind." You might be asking, "What is a sound mind?" and rightfully so, if you have found yourself in a desert and feel desperate. The word for "sound mind" is taken from the Greek word *sophroneo*. It is a compound of the word *sodzo*, which means "delivered or saved," and the word *phroneo*, which refers to intelligent thinking.[1]

When we put the two words together, the new word means to have a delivered or saved mind. This describes a mind that has been renewed by the Word of God and has been set free to think correctly. We begin to have pure thoughts. When your mind is renewed by the Word of God it is perfectly natural to walk by faith. When you have renewed your mind, obeying every word from God seems perfectly logical and natural. You begin to walk in the knowledge of your salvation that was totally paid in full by Jesus Christ on the cross.

If you are having a problem with anger and your tongue as you go through this desert or trial, read and study the first three chapters in the book of James. Begin to memorize scriptures. This brings the Word from your head to your heart. The connection between the head and heart are vital to spiritual growth. You must strengthen your spirit man so that you have a pure heart. When you have a pure heart, the Word of God will come up when you encounter daily life.

CONNECTION OF THE HEAD AND HEART

The Bible tells us in Hebrews 8:1–9:28 that the New Covenant is a better covenant, established by a better Mediator, and established on better promises (Hebrews 8:6). God will write His law on the heart, not just on a tablet of stone. The writer of Hebrews teaches us the law of connection with the head and heart.

In Hebrews 8:1, we learn that our High Priest (Jesus Christ) is seated at the right hand of God the Father and is praying for us. This gives us great assurance once we know who we are in Christ through salvation. Salvation gives you deliverance from sin, salvation from hell, divine protection, preservation, healing, wholeness, and complete soundness of mind. Praise God! He has given us all we will ever need to withstand every fiery dart or attack from the enemy. When we read the Word and it gets into our heart and head, we begin to think what God says and thinks about every situation. We trust Him and believe His Word. We find our confidence in Him.

CHAPTER 40

TOTAL TRUST AND CONFIDENCE

Faith in God

After seeing the well in your desert, the memories of the long nights with nothing but you and your thoughts of desperation will soon fade away as you see the glimpse of day and the *instant awareness* of God's hand in every detail of your life. The apostle Paul said, "I have been crucified with Christ and I no longer live, but Christ lives in me" (Galatians 2:20, NIV). Do you consider your body His and not your own? When we lay down our rights and surrender our will for His, He blesses us in the most extraordinary ways to make us constantly aware of His abiding presence. He blesses us by giving us great ability to see and hear Him. Knowing Him is the greatest blessing of all!

As you share your miracle story of what God has done in your life, you will be a blessing to others. God will continue to give you new and fresh testimonies as you continue your walk in this life. Look for opportunities to share the love of Christ and how He has helped you make it through whatever trial or difficulty you have faced.

You learn that God goes before you and makes every crooked place straight. He opens doors that no man can shut and brings you before kings. He promises us in His Word, "When you go through deep waters, I will be with you. When you go through rivers of difficulty, you will not drown.

When you walk through the fire of oppression, you will not be burned up; the flames will not consume you" (Isaiah 43:2, NLT). I tell people I have walked through the fire and my hair doesn't even smell of smoke.

The Bible says, "Weeping may last through the night, but joy comes with the morning" (Psalm 30:5, NLT). The suffering in the desert will not last forever. God will not leave you in the place of suffering. He will never forsake you. He didn't forsake me, and I can tell you He won't forsake you either.

It may seem like an eternity of pain in the beginning, but each new day will behold a more radiant beauty when you keep your eyes fixed on Jesus. You will soon look at the situation, and it will seem like a movie because the pain will be gone and you will learn to rejoice in what Christ has done for you and is doing through you. Keep your confidence in Him. Don't be silent. Unless you tell your story, how will they know? Don't waste your desert. Become the treasure God made you and step out to give Him glory! Remember that the person who puts his confidence in the Lord "shall be like a tree planted by the waters, Which spreads out its roots by the river, And will not fear when heat comes; But his leaf shall be green, And it will not be anxious in the year of drought, Nor will cease yielding fruit" (Jeremiah 17:8, NKJV). When we place our trust in God rather than in ourselves, we will become stable in Him.

The most important thing God taught me was to place my total trust and confidence in Him. He taught me and showed me by example that He was the greatest encourager. He showed me by changing the entire order of a church service that He was close to the brokenhearted. The Bible tells us plainly that we will have trouble in life. He also tells us, "Thus says the Lord: Cursed [with great evil] is the strong man who trusts in and relies on frail man, making weak [human] flesh his arm, and whose mind and heart turn aside from the Lord" (Jeremiah 17:5, AMP). The Bible also says in verse six: "For he shall be like a shrub or a person naked and destitute in the desert; and he shall not see any good come, but shall dwell in the parched places in the wilderness, in an uninhabited salt land" (Jeremiah 17:6, AMP). Remember to keep your relationships in balance and trust God for everything. Love people and trust God. Love God with your whole heart, mind, and soul and learn to lean on Him for understanding. Don't ever put anyone on a pedestal above God. God must be first in your life. Choose to walk out of the desert by placing your total trust, faith, and confidence in God. You are a priceless treasure in the hand of God.

EXPECT A MIRACLE

Choose to expect a miracle from God! Remember, expectation is a seed. Expectation is an act of faith where you know your miracle has already occurred in the spirit realm and you are waiting and watching for it to happen in the natural. There is always a natural manifestation for what is going on in the spirit. Learn to pay attention and expect God to move on your behalf! Deep down in your heart, you know that God is at work on your specific problem and knows every detail.

Plan your days and organize your life around your expected miracle. Talk about it and believe it. Expecting God to move on your behalf places you in position to receive from God because He promises to turn everything out for your good and His glory. You must only believe. Have faith in God to receive your needed miracle in the midst of the desert. The Bible says, "But without faith it is impossible to please him: for he that cometh to God must believe that he is, and that he is a rewarder of them that diligently seek him" (Hebrews 11:6).

CHAPTER 41

GOD ACHIEVED THE VICTORY

What Does God Do in Response to Our Faith?

Let's take a look at what God did in response to Moses's faith. First, let's take an overview of being in the desert. Can you imagine how Moses must have felt with two million angry people? Have you ever been out to eat in a restaurant with a group of angry people? It feels like a tight place and is not much fun! Moses was obviously in a tight place, a wonderful place to reveal character, grace, and faith. Moses found himself in a place where only God could rescue him. Have you ever felt that way? The depths of despair that come from betrayal, abandonment, abuse, failure in business, looking at wrong choices when you had plenty of warnings, to health issues, can leave you feeling desperate and all alone. It is in these times that God shows Himself strong on our behalf. He waits for us to run to Him.

When we find ourselves in a corner, our hearts are truly exposed. Our greatest temptation will be to find an escape route or the nearest exit that will appear to get us out of the dilemma. You may wake up in the middle of a divorce and just wish God would send you another man to take care of everything. It is in this very place that God wants to show Himself strong on your behalf. He wants you to totally trust Him. He desires that you have faith in Him.

Often Satan will set up an exit strategy to get us to sin against God and His ways. The enemy of our souls offers an easy way out with a deadly trap that is skillfully and deceitfully hidden from view. When we are under attack and in the heat of stress in the desert, we don't hear or see clearly. What options do you have in the spot you have found yourself?

The man who ran out on his wife and had an affair may secretly wish he had sought marriage counseling but has too much pride to admit it and repent. Perhaps we think we can tell one more lie to find our way out of difficulty. Cheating on exams in school or falsifying documents can also be a temporary means of escape. Running from life's problems is not the answer. Turning to God is the answer.

You might be a couple trying to save money before the wedding day, and the enemy tempts you to move in together to save money on the apartment or buy a house together before the wedding. These are subtle traps of the enemy against God's ways. Adultery may appear to be a means of escape, but ends up in divorce, loss of family, and children with damaged emotions. Being in a tight place reveals what is in our heart and reveals our character.

God uses our circumstances to test our character. This is where we really get to see our own personal maturity level. Sometimes it is not a pretty picture to see either.

Moses passed his test in the desert when he chose to pray and seek God rather than panic. He remembered what he had previously learned from earlier conflicts with Pharaoh: situations or circumstances that are totally out of our control are firmly in God's hands. Reflect for a minute while Moses and his people were trapped with the Red Sea in front of them, the mountains surrounding, and the strongest army on earth following behind them. If he had chosen to react as any man might, Moses might have cowered down and told Pharaoh that he and his people would be slaves forever if he would just let them live. He also could have gone into panic mode, fallen apart emotionally, and resigned.

Have you ever felt like resigning from your job, marriage, or just plain life? If this is where you find yourself, you do not walk alone! God is with you. Choose to respond wisely. Let's see how Moses responded.

Moses responded, not by looking ahead to the sea, nor by looking behind to the huge cloud of dust from the army; but he looked up, to God. Jesus did the same thing when he fed the multitudes using the few fish and loaves of bread. He looked up. We must choose to look up! *Are you looking up?*

I am quite sure Moses remembered the promises of the past. God had told Abraham the Israelites would be in the land of Egypt four hundred years and then they would be brought out to go into the land of Canaan. The time was up. He remembered God's Word to him, so he knew God had to preserve His people because God's reputation was at stake.

Moses was also encouraged by the promises of the present. He heard God's voice, "Why are you crying out to me? Tell the Israelites to move on. Raise your staff and stretch out your hand over the sea to the water so that the Israelites can go through the sea on dry ground" (Exodus 14:15–16, NIV). God had a plan that I am quite sure never entered the mind of Moses.

Several things happened that day. First, the Egyptians would be totally wiped out. The Israelites would never have to face Pharaoh again and would never have to look again into the face of his angry men. They would never feel the pain in the heat baking bricks in the hot sun.

Second, God would be glorified through this event as no one could have pulled this off, but God. "The Egyptians will know that I am the LORD, when I gain glory through Pharaoh, his chariots and horsemen" (Exodus 14:18, NIV). God desired that His people have a good night's sleep and rest before marching through the sea, so He sent the pillar of cloud from the front of the nation to the back of them to provide a shield between them and the Egyptians. We see the Angel of the Lord change from being a guide to a guardian (Exodus 14:19). When any situation calls for the impossible, and we feel like we are up against a sea or wilderness, God is always present.

What exactly did God ask the people to do during this time? It seems He asked them to "stand firm" through waiting and resting. They were to prepare themselves to see God at work as they had never seen before. "Moses answered the people, 'Do not be afraid. Stand firm and you will see the deliverance the LORD will bring you today. The Egyptians you see today you will never see again. The LORD will fight for you; you need only to be still'" (Exodus 14:13–14, NIV).

This was not a time to run away, nor a time to start a fight. Their mouths were to be quiet. It was not a time to scream and shout all their complaints to their friends. This was obviously God's move and not theirs. He had led them into a place that felt like a corner or a dead end with no way of escape. The only hope they had was God Himself. The people had sprinkled the blood on their doorposts in Egypt and had packed for the long journey that lay ahead of them for the long trip to Canaan.

There are some tight places in life when the bills are unpaid, when the spouse ran off, when your business partner shafted you out of millions, to the death of a spouse, or a bad medical report. The only thing we can do is look up!

Apparently, Moses cried out to the Lord more than he needed as the Lord asked him why he was crying out. It came down to the wire and was a time for Moses to act (Exodus 14:15–16). Can you imagine the trembling legs as Moses stretched out his staff over the sea—the same staff he used to herd sheep—and all of a sudden, the miracle began to happen as the wind blew and the waters parted for them to walk over? What seemed like an ordinary staff became an extraordinary, supernatural, staff of God.

In the morning, the Israelites encountered walls of water on either side, but Moses commanded them to go and they obeyed immediately. I would imagine they all had some fear, but it was obvious the plan of God was being made evident to them. What did God do in response to Moses's faith? He confused the enemy and destroyed them. The Egyptians obviously were unaware they would be destroyed as they raced toward the Israelites. The Bible says in Psalm 77:16–20 that God caused a rainstorm with lightning and thunder, and an earthquake. God was orchestrating every detail. "He made the wheels of their chariots come off so that they had difficulty driving. And the Egyptians said, 'Let's get away from the Israelites! The LORD is fighting for them against Egypt'" (Exodus 14:25, NIV). While the enemy was destroyed, the Israelites were safe on dry land.

Why did God do this? "Nevertheless He saved them for the sake of His name, That He might make His power known. Thus He rebuked the Red Sea and it dried up; and He led them through the deeps as through the wilderness" (Psalm 106:8–9, NASB). In hours of confusion, times of weeping or screaming, turbulent times of distress and loss of hope, the Egyptians finally knew that Jehovah was God. They came to this conclusion too late for their own personal benefit, but God still received glory by humiliating their false god and proving that He is the One True and Only God.

God did this for the Israelites so they would have a new song in their hearts. A song of deliverance filled their hearts and mouths. God also did this to preserve His own integrity. His enemies saw justice and His power. Meanwhile, His chosen friends saw His amazing love and faithfulness. Still today, we marvel at the wondrous works of God.

Has God led you into a tight place? Perhaps you lost your entire life savings. Maybe an investment deal in a new business went south. The places where we find ourselves in life are not always because we have sin in our lives, but sometimes divinely orchestrated by the will of God. The Lord sometimes leads us on a path with detours and dry places to show us what is in our own heart. He desires to prove Himself faithful. There are no tight places for God. There is no desert big enough that God can't open your eyes to see His well of provision.

Sometimes we are in a mess due to disobeying God's warnings and instructions in the Bible. Other times, we just want to complain and remain, rather than moving forward and trusting God. What about the woman who chooses to have a baby without being married or a teenager who gets pregnant? What about the man who is caught cheating on his income taxes or leaves his business partner holding millions of dollars in debt that was borrowed solely for his benefit? What about the woman who is having an affair with her best friend's husband? Oh, what a tangled web people weave. I remember last year at Christmas walking through Hobby Lobby and seeing towels. One that caught my eye was: Don't Get Your Tinsel Tangled. These kinds of entanglements are due to our own rebellion.

In desperation, some turn to alcohol, recreational drugs or prescription drugs, or lavish pleasure. These attempts are all delusional and actually compound our problems. These means of escape are traps of the enemy to further ensnare us. We all know people who have made wrong choices too many times. We have all made wrong choices! When people make wrong choices on a regular basis, they begin to feel hopeless and give up, getting more and more confused, feeling there is no way out of the mess.

When in a mess we have created ourselves, the lesson we must learn is that God provides a way of escape. Even when we have disobeyed God and it is clearly our fault, God stands ready to help us. Remember the prodigal son in the Bible. The Father stood afar off watching. He was waiting for his son to return. The Bible says, "No temptation has overtaken you but such as common to man; and God is faithful, who will not allow you to be tempted beyond what you are able, but with the temptation will provide the way of escape also, that you may be able to endure it" (1 Corinthians 10:13, NASB).

What is His way of escape? God gives us the grace to do the right thing and then empowers us to learn to live with the consequences. God walks us through whatever mess we find ourselves. He does not promise we will be exempt from pain and the troubles in life, but that He will walk with us through the heat and fire and we will not be burned with flames. No matter where you find yourself today, if you are still breathing, it is not too late. Find a trusted counselor, friend, or minister that will help you take the steps necessary so you can succeed in life. Cry out to God in repentance and ask Him to give you a new heart. If you are a Christian and find yourself in a mess, cry out to God in repentance for His wisdom and intervention.

Right decisions are most often the most difficult. It might be ending that adulterous relationship to reconcile your family to coming clean on a matter where you need to stand up and face a friend you betrayed in business. You might have been hiding something for years and you feel the Lord gently tugging at your heart today. It is you, my precious reading friend, to whom God is speaking. Don't miss His touch. When He reaches down from heaven and touches our mess, He gives us a message to give others hope.

When David committed adultery and murder, God was ready to forgive. When Adam and Eve sinned, God was ready to redeem. When Daniel was in the lions' den, God was with him. When we repent and cry out to Him, He hears our prayers. Start by saying, "Jesus!"

Sometimes God allows us to stay in the desert for an extended period of time so we won't make the wrong choices again. He wants us to move forward in Him. He wants us to take His Word in our hands and allow God to renew our minds as we read His Word. He wants us to focus on Him. Whatever we speak about gets magnified and becomes the center of our focus. We must learn to magnify God instead of our problems. When we finally surrender our entire life to God, we soon realize every situation or life circumstance that is out of our hands is in His! No matter how high the mountain may appear or how deep the water of your Red Sea, God still stands with you waiting for you to cry out to Him and obey His instructions. God knows right where you are. He wants to get Egypt and bondage out of you. He wants you to learn the valuable lesson of saying what He says and stop rehearsing the pain and past. You are positioned for training, under His keeping power, and in His time.

"I will sing to the Lord, for He is highly exalted; The horse and its rider He has hurled into the sea. The LORD is my strength and song, And He has become my salvation; This is my God, and I will praise Him; My father's God, and I will extol Him. The Lord is a warrior; the Lord is His name" (Exodus 15:1–3, NASB).

THE DEAD, RED, OR MED

What is the dead, red, or med? The Dead Sea has no life in it. There is so much salt in the Dead Sea that you actually float on it. The Red Sea appeared to be an obstacle to the Israelites until God showed His miraculous power for them and provided a way of escape. An obstacle can also be used as an instrument.

The Mediterranean is a beautiful sea and a place of rest. I remember on one of our trips to Israel, Jordan, and Eilat, we had a wonderful experience of rest and peace at a resort. Reflecting back over the three bodies of water, you can see God was getting Egypt out of the Israelites so that when they got to the place where they could see Egypt, they would not dare want to go back.

In the late 1980s many international scientists actually chose the Red Sea as one of the Seven Wonders of the Underwater World. The Red Sea is known as one of the two saltiest bodies of water anywhere in the world, second only to the Dead Sea, which is a short distance away between Israel and Jordan.

The Red Sea touches several countries altogether including Egypt, Israel, Jordan, and more. There is something very spectacular about the Red Sea. The water is world-renowned for its clear blue water, its shiny beaches, and its very exotic marine life. In fact, researchers claim that there are over 1,000 invertebrate species and 200 corals that populate the Red Sea, not to mention over 300 types of sharks.

Speaking of marine life, all underwater creatures and desert life are protected by law, since some of the creatures are endangered species. Breaking these regulations could result in massive international fines.

When we stay under the blood of Jesus and under the protection of God through the Water of His Word, we too are protected by God. We have to choose to dig in the Word of God, stay in the Word so our minds are transformed through the renewing of our minds, and keep our focus on Jesus. Then we become salt and light to the whole world; a living epistle and a life changed by the power of the blood and the cross of Jesus Christ.

We are born in sin and spiritually dead until we confess Jesus as Lord. *Confess* means "to say out of your mouth." The finished work on the cross and the blood of Jesus cover us completely when we become born again. God sees us through the precious blood of His Son Jesus. Become a living epistle read by all men. You may be the only Bible some people ever read (2 Corinthian 3:2).

CHAPTER 42

DISAPPOINTMENT

The Test of Faith

The word *disappointment* is in everyone's vocabulary. We have all experienced disappointment. People will disappoint us. Think of the people you know who have personally walked through abandonment, affairs, adultery, cancer, financial betrayal and collapse; to the woman who was convinced that her husband would never cheat on her, only to learn he was having an affair with a relative. What about the man who was married for twenty years to learn his wife had been having an affair for seven years; can you imagine his pain? What about the child that was raised in church but grew up and made bad choices?

Parents are disappointed in children. Employers are sometimes disappointed in their staff, and the staff can also be disappointed in their boss. We can also be disappointed in circumstances. We can also feel disappointed in God when we don't get what we prayed for or things don't turn out as planned. The Israelites suffered severe disappointment. (See Exodus 15:22–27.) Soon after their miracle at the Red Sea, their song turned to mourning, and their music to murmuring and complaining. The mountaintop experience set them up for ultimate despair. Walking through the hot desert reduced their supply of water, and it seemed there was no water in sight. Scouts were sent out and came back with negative reports.

Imagine the heat of the day and the tiredness in their eyes from the blazing sun. The wind that blew against them probably felt like a furnace as well. Anxiety increased and they assumed God did not care until they spotted an oasis in the desert.

Their tongues were parched and the water was too bitter to swallow. The Bible says, "And when they came to Marah, they could not drink the waters of Marah, for they were bitter: therefore it was named Marah. And the people murmured against Moses, saying, 'What shall we drink?'" (Exodus 15:23–24).

Then the murmuring, complaining, and grumbling began. They felt they had been deceived by Moses and God. Why on earth had He led them into a desert to die? *What was God's purpose in this?* The Bible says, "There He made for them a statute and an ordinance, and there he proved them" (Exodus 15:25). This was a test to reveal their level of commitment. It was also a revelation of what was in their hearts.

Disappointment reveals what is in our hearts, reveals our character, and lets us know who we really are. It is like looking in a mirror to face oneself. You will either grow in faith or grumble in doubt, anger, and unbelief. Who led the Israelites to Marah? Yes, it was God! They were right in the center of God's will. Have you ever felt like you prayed and stayed, you did everything you knew to do, but the business or marriage did not turn out the way you had hoped? No matter what we have done or not done, God is still standing by to help us make the best of our failures and disappointments.

Disappointments test our focus, our faith, and our faithfulness

Let's take an in-depth look. Whether it is the thirst of the Israelites, or the single mom who is lonely and afraid, or the workaholic who is married to his job, the temptation is always the same. When we place our hopes in something we think will meet our need, we have lost focus. The more our hearts are consumed by what we think we need and want, the greater the possibility of disappointment.

When we put our hope in a person or a leader instead of Jesus Christ, we have lost our focus. I am sure you have heard, "Don't put all your eggs in one basket." You can put everything in God. He will never disappoint you.

Circumstances and people bring disappointment. Knowing that God has the best plan brings peace and contentment when we choose to surrender to His will. You may have married the perfect man who seemed to be a dream, and it turned into a nightmare. Disappointment is one of God's ways of showing us we have idols in our life.

Asaph was an Old Testament prophet who was envious of the wicked, but when he saw his life from God's perspective and viewpoint he wrote, "Whom have I in heaven but thee? and there is none upon earth that I desire beside thee. My flesh and my heart faileth; but God is the strength of my heart, and my portion forever" (Psalm 73:25–26). Let's check our focus and learn to see from God's point of view. Thirst in the desert of life's experiences will either drive us to God or make us angry, and sometimes both. God reveals the true state of our hearts when we feel like we are being deprived of some basic human need.

Disappointments test our faith

What do you do when you begin to feel bitterness in your heart? Can you imagine how Moses must have felt as he was surrounded by all those angry people blaming him for winding up in the desert without water? He chose to shut them out and started talking to God. This is a very valuable lesson. As I was sharing with a precious lady today about shutting people out and talking to God, I reflected on Moses. Moses cried out to the Lord. (Read Exodus 15:25–26.) God showed Moses a tree, and he threw it into the waters, and the waters became sweet.

Moses believed God and he did not care if the people did or not. He was sold out to God, no matter what. He chose to look up. Prayer puts us in touch with God. He has all the resources we will ever need. When Moses started praying, a miracle started happening. You see, God opened his eyes to see a tree he was to put in the water. God often changes our circumstances in response to prayer. *The greatest miracle of all is when God changes us in the midst of our circumstances.*

Throwing the tree in the water was a symbolic act, similar to Moses holding his staff or rod over the Red Sea. God used what was in Moses's hands. God changed the waters of Marah simply because He chose to do so for His people. Bitter waters were made sweet. God touches our bitter circumstances and makes us aware of His presence. The sweet water of His Word brings cleansing and refreshing.

God touches our circumstances and changes things for our benefit. I remember as a young girl, I worked in the evenings after school in my junior year of high school to save money for my first car. I found a car I really wanted and was on my way to purchase it with cash. The car dealership knew I was on my way also. When I arrived, I learned someone had come just before me and bought the car I had wanted to purchase. I learned a couple weeks later that the car had caught on fire with the new owner. I realized God was showing me His protection through blocking me from buying a car with a problem. This may seem small to you, but this is the love of God. Sometimes when we don't get what we think we want, it is God's way of saving us from something far worse.

Disappointments test our faithfulness

God gave specific regulations regarding the law in the Old Testament concerning such things as what the Israelites were to eat, how they were to dispense with waste, and how they were to cleanse themselves. God promised if they would obey His instructions, they would be healed and exempt from the diseases that plagued the Egyptians. God was showing them He would spare them from disease in the desert.

You might be disappointed that someone dear to you died. Healing was paid for on the cross. We will all be healed physically when we receive our resurrection bodies. Where there is darkness, God shines His light. Where there is a wound, God brings healing. He stands with us as the Great Physician, enabling us to make our spiritual journey in this life. God uses our disappointments to test our obedience. There comes a time when we all must die, unless we go in the Rapture, so we need to make sure of our salvation.

CHAPTER 43

CHOICE

The Two Trees

There are two most important trees in the Bible. The first was obviously the tree of the knowledge of good and evil in the Garden of Eden. When Adam and Eve partook of the fruit from that tree in disobedience to God's instruction, the whole stream of life became bitter. Sin has contaminated everything in life since that time.

The second tree is the cross. God used this tree for blessing. It is also the tree that reverses the curse that the tree in the Garden of Eden caused. God's tree absorbed the curse of sin and purified its waters. Paul spoke of that tree: "Christ has redeemed us from the curse of the law, having become a curse for us (for it is written, 'Cursed is everyone who hangs on a tree') that the blessing of Abraham might come to the Gentiles in Christ Jesus, that we might receive the promise of the Spirit through faith" (Galatians 3:13–14, NKJV).

Interestingly enough, Jesus was offered wine mingled with myrrh (which in Hebrew is *marah*, "bitter"). This was used as a sedative to alleviate pain. Christ said no because He wanted to die fully aware. *What does the cross do?* Like the tree used by Moses, the tree that was used as the cross takes life with all its bitterness and makes it sweet. We have the precious fruit through Jesus's death, our crucified Redeemer.

Sin brings destruction. David made a parallel between sickness and sin: "Who pardons all your iniquities; Who heals all your diseases" (Psalm 103:3, NASB). The Prophet Isaiah when speaking of the nation Israel said, "From the sole of the foot even to the head There is nothing sound in it, Only bruises, welts and raw wounds, Not pressed out or bandaged, Nor softened with oil" (Isaiah 1:6, NASB). *How does the cross make our bitter waters sweet?* When we accept Jesus as Lord, our sins are forgiven, and our consciences come to rest. He speaks the word that we might be cleansed and made whole (nothing missing, nothing broken). He heals the brokenhearted: "He heals the brokenhearted, And binds up their wounds. He counts the number of stars; He gives names to all of them" (Psalm 147:3–4, NASB).

The one and only true and living God who counts the stars is the God who heals our souls. The world runs to and fro searching for healing through attaining massive amounts of wealth, the latest new home, to the latest new piece of technology that money can buy. Money cannot buy the peace and fulfillment that only God can give. I find it very interesting that in the Garden we have been told that the piece of fruit from the forbidden tree was perhaps an apple. I find it very interesting that one of the companies that always have the latest and newest piece of technology is also Apple. Technology is an awesome tool, but can also be used as a distraction. I remember hearing a friend of mine telling me people came and stood outside the door of that store, lined up for hours before it actually opened, just to buy the newest device. If only we sought Jesus in that same way.

If you forget your phone, do you turn around and go back home to get it? Do you carry the Bible with you wherever you go? Do you have God's Word hidden in your heart that no matter what happens, that is the first thing that comes to mind? If not, it is time to get back to the basics and foundation that God has given us through His Son Jesus.

After Marah, the Israelites came to Elim, where there were twelve springs of water and seventy date palms (Exodus 15:27). The thirsty Israelites discovered one spring for each of the twelve tribes and enough fruit for everyone to enjoy. I understand that on a map you can't actually see Marah from Elim, but God knew and had it planned all along.

God knows every detail and every turn your life will take. He knows how to quench our thirst. When I was so deeply wounded from abuse, abandonment, betrayal, and damaged emotions from all the traumatic events I had experienced, God Himself sought me out and taught me Himself. He taught me I was valuable and a priceless treasure to Him. Even when the world didn't think so, God did and still does! He takes our lives that are broken and fixes them so He can use our story to bring Him glory.

I have written this book from the instruction of the Lord and pray that as you read it, you too, find that God has a great plan for your life. He can take the bitter waters and make them sweet. He can see a great future, even when you see everything as pain. Your disappointment might very well be a place where God reveals Himself to you and shows you that instead of disappointment it is a divine appointment with the God who loves you! God leads us from the desert to refreshing in Him!

CHAPTER 44

GOD IS NOT CAUGHT OFF GUARD

He Is All Knowing

God is not caught off guard by anything that you have experienced or are currently walking through in the desert. God's love is permanent and He is all knowing. God always protects, but He does not always prevent pain. Pain is our greatest teacher. Pain informs us something is very wrong. God can use pain to bring humility into our lives and makes us ever aware of our constant need of Him.

Most people don't recognize their need until they walk through a desert place. God desires that we choose Him. God uses our circumstances in this world to perfect us and make us like Him. The more we choose to do the right thing, the more our fleshly, worldly nature is crucified.

You can know God in your head and not know Him in your heart. You may have heard all about Him, but not really have a personal, intimate relationship with Him. I always heard a saying, "Don't miss heaven by eighteen inches," which is supposedly the distance between your head and heart. God calls out to us from behind the lattice of grace inviting us to choose Him with our own free will. He is a gentleman. He desires we choose Him and His ways that are always best for us in His divine plan. God does not cause pain, but He uses pain to purge us, purify us, and place us in position to prosper in knowing Him and His ways.

Hell will be filled with people who heard about God but never knew Him. Sometimes pain is used to show us the places in us that need to be healed and hardened areas in the heart that need to be softened. He is the great heart surgeon. He desires to remove the poison of bitterness in the heart that comes when we choose not to forgive those who have wronged us and ourselves. Choose to believe God! (See Ephesians 3:18; John 3:16.) It has been said that John 3:16 is the hope diamond of the Bible. God is more concerned about us being born again and knowing Him than He is about our comfort. We are a precious jewel to Him, a priceless treasure, a royal diadem in His hand!

CHAPTER 45

GOD CREATED YOU
TO BE AN EAGLE

Those who hope in the Lord will renew their strength. They
will soar on wings like eagles...

—ISAIAH 40:3, NIV

The costly price for your breakthrough has been lovingly paid, in full, by Jesus Christ on the cross. It is His plan for you to live victoriously as you come to Him as beloved sons and daughters. He desires a deep, intimate relationship with each of His children. Learn to walk in the fullness of your rich inheritance as a co-heir with Christ.

All people are searching for something. Most women are searching for a man at some time in their life. Men are searching for a love relationship as well. We must learn to keep our focus on God. That void or place in your heart that has a deep longing for something is really a longing for God, and only He can truly fill it. When we learn to seek Him and His kingdom, God delights in giving us the desires of our hearts. Our desires begin to line up with His righteousness and kingdom purposes.

The Psalmist David says, "Bless the LORD, O my soul; And all that is within me, *bless* His holy name! Bless the LORD, O my soul, And forget not all His benefits; Who forgives all your iniquities, Who heals all your diseases; Who redeems your life from the pit, Who crowns you with lovingkindness and compassion; Who satisfies your years with good things, So that your youth is renewed like the eagle" (Psalm 103:1–5, NASB).

God shows us that He pardons. We must put our past shame or blame behind. God heals. We must choose to become healthy and be set free from old wounds. God redeems. God redeems your abilities and personality. He has hidden treasures in you that are just waiting to be revealed. You will see it yourself. God crowns us with gifts and a place to serve. God satisfies. We will begin to feel satisfied and fulfilled as you and I live out God's plan for our lives.

When we walk in the Spirit, we are confident in God (Psalm 56:9; 118:6). We chase after God to know Him more and seek to find God's will (John 10:14; Romans 12:2; Ephesians 5:17). We have a willingness to be self-sacrificing (Matthew 20:25–28; Luke 9:23). We search and find God's ways and methods and we obey them (Psalm 40:8; 143:10). We become a servant of all and are motivated by love for God and man (Mark 10:42–45; 1 John 4:7–21). We are dependent upon God (Isaiah 42:1; John 15:5) and are empowered by the Holy Spirit (Acts 1:8). He raises us up in a place to serve so we can lead others through their desert place to find His shelter and healing in the sandstorms of life (1 Peter 5:2–3).

Natural leaders are self-confident, know all the right people, and are ambitious, making their own decisions. Natural born leaders also enjoy commanding others and are motivated by self-interest. They are very independent and use their personality to their benefit. They sometimes operate like a drill-sergeant or a rancher. All natural-born instincts and skills are far better when submitted to the leadership and power of the Holy Spirit. Learn to submit your gifts, talents, and personality to the leadership of the Holy Spirit.

Once you have reached your place to serve others, which right now might seem like a dream out of your reach, you must always remember where you came from and who your true source is—God. This is a key distinction between people walking in the Spirit and those using their natural skills. Remember to always lead others like a loving parent and not like a boss.

God will bring people by you that are in the desert. He will train you to make it through so you can help others. We have all heard people say, "Just get over it," but that is not the process of healing. You know from your own past experiences there are things in life that happen that take time to heal. When you begin to step out in God's plan for your life, He will make sure the resources are available for you. He is our great provider! Maintain the vision and goal God has placed in your heart and you will begin to soar like the eagle in God's plan for your life. Keep God in first place in your life.

We want to have a childlike heart to believe God at His every Word. We want to be full of faith to lead others. The Bible tells us in Isaiah 11:6: "A little child shall lead them." I have a piece of art with a little blonde-haired girl walking with a bucket of water with this scripture underneath. This also reminds me of the woman at the well in Samaria who led her city to meet Jesus.

LOOKING AHEAD

Moses came down from the mountain, and his faced glowed as he had been in the holy presence of the Lord. When you learn to look ahead and hold your head high again, you will begin to see clearly, more than ever before. You become sensitive to the Holy Spirit and His leading and will be able to discern those who are your real friends. Those that stick beside you and pray with you through the desert are God's chosen friends. A true friend considers your feelings above their own. They will tell you the truth in love if they see you going down a wrong path. They will encourage you and love you through the process. They want you to succeed.

God lets us know just as He ministered to us, He will use you to minister to others. The Lord comforts and ministers to each of us through pain and suffering so we can offer the same to others (2 Corinthians 1:3–4). Pain actually positions and aligns us in need of God (PAIN). It is in the place of pain that most people pursue God.

We then go through purging and pruning where God works the things out of us that are not of Him. He prunes us by doing surgery in our hearts as we submit to His loving touch, for He is the Great Physician. He positions us strategically so we can grow and develop His character and His ways of doing things. We then have our priorities in line with His will so we can move forward in life with His purposes in mind, operating in purity of heart, with passion and empowered with purpose to complete our course here on earth for God's kingdom. When we have walked through the pain, we are then able to see and hear clearly. We learn to trust God for everything. *Our life becomes one of producing proficiency, progress, professionalism, prosperity, and purpose for God.* We begin to bear much fruit. We have great potential. We are moved with compassion to see and desire to help others through their desert to the well of living water, this man Jesus!

God doesn't heal you to put you up on a shelf. He is the Master and begins to train you Himself. He gives us direction as we learn to continue the process of transformation as we transition from the desert to the oasis of God's unconditional love and provision. God uses the times we walk through affliction, heartbreak, sickness, abandonment, rape, broken relationships, trauma, financial loss, to a host of other ways to get us alone with Him. It is in the quiet alone times with Him that we come to find out just who God is and learn to know who we are in Christ. He walks with us through the valley to the top of the precipices where the lilies of the fields and magnolias blossom. You become a sweet smelling fragrance to all you meet.

I was listening to a minster on the radio today and learned that certain flowers are harvested for perfume in the darkest hours of the night. This is when the flowers naturally produce the most wonderful fragrance. We become a sweet-smelling fragrance when we have walked through a dark valley or season as well. God doesn't waste our pain.

We learn to sit at His feet like Mary did and bask in His holy presence. We learn to like the quiet times hearing the voice of our heavenly Father, and we love to hear his heart beat as we lay our head on His chest. During the last days of my daddy's life that is exactly what we did. I put my head on my daddy's chest so he could touch my head as I listened to his heart and his sweet words. Those words and his touch I will always cherish. We learn to soak in God's Word so that our hearts are so full of the water of His Word that we are not moved or harmed by darts of fire from the enemy. Most importantly, we seek Him with our whole heart and His will. Once you come through the pain and realize God has a great plan in store for you, a new fresh outlook seems to fill your soul. Walking out God's plan for your life brings fulfillment and joy, knowing you have been created by God, on purpose, for a purpose!

No matter where you find yourself now, seek Him with your whole heart. Get connected with a church. Find a pastor or head of women's ministry or men's ministry and learn to serve. It is a privilege and honor that God has bestowed upon each and every one of His children. As you surrender your life to God, you will be activated by the power of the Holy Spirit to do the work of the Father and see the kingdom of God released in your life in a greater way. Get moving!

CHAPTER 46

DOING THINGS WITH GOD

Activate His Power

The key to doing things with God is to surrender your life to Him. You will be activated by the power of the Holy Spirit to do the work of the Father and see the kingdom of God released in your life in a greater way. Learn to do things with God. Are you doing things with God, or are you doing things for God? Are you listening to the sound of His still small voice for direction, or are you running to and fro like the "energizer bunny" that we have most all seen on television? Are you spirit led, or are you running your life like a business, forgetting about relationship with God and people? Don't lose your focus in the desert. Don't lose your focus after you see the well in your desert and start to move forward with God.

You may be a pastor running so fast that you have stopped drinking from the fountain yourself. Stop and minister to the Lord! Spend time in His presence, not just studying for a sermon. Become a pastor of purity! Become people of purity! Choose to stay eternity minded. Choose to stay connected with people of like-minded faith in God. When you choose to stay connected and get moving, God will do amazing things in and through your life as you trust Him for the details and quit trying to figure everything out. Stop controlling everything, and instead of manipulating circumstances, learn to trust God even with the stoplights that so easily irritate people and put you in a position to wait. Learn to wait patiently with God for His perfect timing.

I've got news for you! News flash! God knows better than us. Get back to the basics and learn to simplify your life. Take time for those you love and learn to develop godly relationships with others. We need each other. Don't miss one opportunity for a God-given connection that may be the very pivotal turning point in your life for your destiny and legacy. God uses the least likely people, and oftentimes we will not recognize them at first. Learn to trust God and see through His eyes.

CHAPTER 47

NURTURE YOUR RELATIONSHIP WITH THE LORD

He Knows How to Solve Problems

SLEEP IS A HEALING AGENT

Your body is the temple of the Holy Spirit. Learn to take care of your body when in a desert place. Sleep gives us the ability to rest and be refreshed with new energy. Sleep is the seed for energy that is vital for life. You will learn what your own special needs are for you as an individual.

You don't think properly when you don't get enough sleep. You assess life differently and talk differently when tired. When you choose to stop talking about the pain and what has happened to you and start talking about what God has done in and through you, healing begins.

Sleep is a major role in the healing process while in a desert place. Make a habit of going to bed early to get the proper rest you need. When you are fatigued and washed out, your faith seems to waver. "And He said unto them, Come ye yourselves apart into a desert place, and rest a while: for there were many coming and going, and they had no leisure so much as to eat" (Mark 6:31).

BACK TO THE BASICS

Get back to the basics of nurturing your relationship with the Lord. Remember suffering brings us back to the basics where we learn to trust God at His every word. Suffering leads us to the desert where we get alone with God and learn to be comfortable with Him by ourselves.

We learn to trust in Jesus, trust in God, and depend on His Word. If you never have a problem, you don't know that God can solve it. Most people don't seek God with their whole heart until they walk through a place of suffering, a fiery trial, or find themselves in the desert. Desperate people get desperate for God. "My heart says of you, 'Seek his face!' Your face, Lord I will seek" (Psalm 27:8, NIV).

We become a living testimony of the grace, mercy, and love of God. (See 1 Peter 4:12–18.) Beloved, *don't be surprised* when you walk through a trial. We draw biblical strength for the fiery trials. We learn to please God the Father rather than man. You learn how to respond properly when trials come. Life is living individually for eternity. Life is like a classroom where you never fail your tests. God keeps giving them to you over and over until you pass. A test is a critical examination, observation, or examination. Suffering and trials cause us to stop and look at ourselves. We begin to look in the mirror of God's Word and see who we really are inside. God tests us so we can discover how well we are really doing. How we respond with tests reveals our maturity. The testing of your faith is revealing to you the level of your individual maturity. At the revelation of His glory, you may rejoice. (Keep on rejoicing!)

You can rejoice because you enter into a closer partnership with Christ. God looks at the heart. What's in your heart is what really matters. Paul says in the Word, "That I may know Him and the fellowship of His sufferings" (Philippians 3:10), indicating we don't really know Him until we walk through fiery trials. When we suffer for the cause of Christ, we become more closely linked to Him and understand His thoughts. When we suffer for the cause of Christ, we will receive a future reward.

Learn to hide yourselves in the Word of God that He may refresh you

It is in the hidden place of the heart where God refreshes. God desires that we have sweet communion with Him together by learning to sit at His feet. We set aside and plan a time each day to meet with Him by reading His Word and communing with Him in prayer. Out of this precious and sacred communion comes the blessing of the kingdom of God. *God teaches you how to walk in the Spirit.* Walking in the Spirit may seem supernatural to others around you who are observing, but it is a natural way of living according to God's Word. He promises to teach us how to walk in the Spirit, to know the voice of the Spirit, and how to perceive the signs of the Spirit. It is out of this place where His glory flows, even as a river. Chase after God. Get desperate for God.

God's plan of redemption also includes hiding you from the greatest turmoil and attack of the enemy

His Son Jesus paid the price on the cross. When we apply the blood of Jesus, by faith, the angel of death has to pass over us. Destruction has to go. Learn to daily apply the blood of Jesus to your mind, will, and emotions; to your health, relationships, family, and finances. The blood of Jesus is the secret place. He is a refuge, our place of safety, provision, and protection.

God knows how to solve your problem. Bring your problems to Him, and He will show you the way of resolution and direct your steps. Your corresponding action is to trust Him, refuse to allow doubt to enter your mind, walk through fear, and don't doubt God's willingness or ability to bring you through every desert. Nurture your mind with the Word of God. Nurture your faith. The Bible says, "A man's heart plans his way, but the Lord directs his steps" (Proverbs 16:9).

CHAPTER 48

VITAL STEPS

Stop Talking and Start Praying

There are vital steps to living in God's love and His plan. Pray for your enemies and ask God to bless them. Praying for those who have wronged you can lead them to a place of true repentance and realization of the harm they are causing you and others. Pray for God to bless those who have hurt you, misused, abused, and ridiculed you. The Bible says, "But I tell you, Love your enemies and pray for those who persecute you" (Matthew 5:44). You are praying for God to make Himself known to them. The Bible also says, "Invoke blessings upon and pray for the happiness of those who curse you, implore God's blessing (favor) upon those who abuse you [who revile, reproach, disparage, and high-handedly misuse you]" (Luke 6:28).

Another great verse is Romans 12:14: "Bless those who persecute you [who are cruel in their attitude toward you]; bless and do not curse them." As you are praying for them, you will find God's love being shed abroad in your heart. You cannot truly hate anyone you are praying for, and this will aid in your healing.

You must also choose to stop talking about the problem and pray God's Word, which is the answer. If you continue rehearsing the pain, you are sowing seeds that continue to reap a harvest. There is a time for talking about it, but if you are rehearsing pain that is not fresh, you are keeping the door to the enemy open and blocking your healing. Start thanking God for your healing.

The secret of success is concentration. Keep your focus on Christ. The cause of failure is broken focus. Satan tries to keep you focused on your past. He tempts you to react in the flesh so you miss your future. He comes to emotionally cripple you to the point of devastation.

Examine your life and those you connect with on a regular basis. **Disconnect from every distraction. Fix your eyes on Jesus Christ.** Choose to visualize your future so bright that you forget the past. The Bible says, "Only be thou strong and very courageous, that thou mayest observe to do according to all the law, which Moses my servant commanded thee: turn not from it to the right hand or to the left, that thou mayest prosper whithersoever thou goest" (Joshua 1:7, KJV). As your soul begins to prosper, every other area of your life will as well.

After you have reached a place of healing and find someone with whom to share what God has done for you, you will begin to feel His love shed abroad in your heart and true compassion for others. You will become like Jesus to others. People will be able to sense His very presence when they meet you. Our destiny is to be so much like Jesus that people cannot tell the difference as we live and interact with a world that is blind to His love, mercy, and grace. God wants us to live in Him. When we know Him, we will live and act like He does in this fallen world.

When we come to really know Him, people will be able to tell a difference. We will begin to live as He would. We will respond rather than react. If you are still reacting, then you are not walking in the Spirit but in your carnal flesh.

Knowing Him is more than quoting scripture and going to church on Sunday or Wednesday night. We are a priceless treasure in the hand of God. We are the apple of His eye and are very precious in His sight. We all have been bruised by the fall in the Garden of Eden. Jesus stopped what He was doing, came to earth, died on the cross, and arose three days later that we might have life. He picked us up on the hill called Calvary and paid the price for our eternity. Choose to share Him with others and how He has helped you through. Talk the answer and not the problem. Share His love with all you meet. Become a person of influence! Love extravagantly! Ask God to teach you how to live in His cloak of humility! Live with a forgiving heart! Be generous and trust God with the outcome! Obey God's every instruction at the slightest whisper at the door of your heart!

CHAPTER 49

GOD'S EXTRAVAGANT LOVE

Open Doors of Opportunity

The central theme of Paul's prayer for us as God's people is that we may know God's love. Paul prays that we may be established in God's love and that we may be able to grasp how wide, how long, how high, and how deep it is. Then Paul concludes by saying, "to know this love that surpasses knowledge..." (Ephesians 3:19, NIV). That is a paradox, isn't it? How can we possibly know love that surpasses knowledge? I know the answer because I have personally experienced God's extravagant love! We do not know it through our intellect, but we know it through the revelation of Scripture, of the Holy Spirit, and by His personal touch in our lives. *The Father reveals His love to us Himself.*

Let's take a final look as we come to the close of this writing by seeing what God also says in a passage that is a parable of Jesus found in Matthew 13:44. It is the parable of the treasure hidden in the field. A parable is a simple story about familiar, material, or earthly things that's purpose is to reveal unseen, eternal, and spiritual things. As we look at the natural things, we can see as if looking into a mirror that reflects what is unseen to the natural eye. We begin to see spiritual things. Jesus proceeds from the known to the unknown to explain to His hearers. This is similar to what I have said earlier about natural manifestations that reveal what is going on in the spiritual world.

The parable reads: "The kingdom of heaven is like treasure hidden in a field. When a man found it, he hid it again, and then in his joy went and sold all he had and bought that field" (Matthew 13:44, NIV). I believe the man who found the treasure is Jesus. The field represents the world. This is also stated in Matthew 13:38 in another parable. The same principle runs through all seven parables that are found in Matthew 13. I believe the treasure is God's people in the world. When the man in the parable discovered treasure in the field, he made a very wise choice and bought the field. He did not run and tell everyone about the hidden treasure. In fact, he hid it. Can you imagine how much competition that would stir up and how many people would have been running to buy that same field? All the man wanted was the treasure in the field. He obviously knew to have the treasure he had to purchase the entire field. The price of the field was costly. It cost him all he had, but he did it with joy because he knew the value of the hidden treasure.

Can you image the local residents making fun of him for spending all he had for a field? Why did he pay such a price for a field full of thorns and thistles? They did not know about the treasure. The only one who knew about the treasure was Jesus! He paid the high price for the whole field in order to obtain all the treasure in the field. The treasure is God's people. The field is the world.

In Titus 2:14, "Who gave himself for us to redeem us from every lawless deed, and to purify for himself a people for His own possession, zealous for good deeds" (NASB). *This is the treasure! A people who have been redeemed from the world: redeemed from wickedness, purified, and made zealous to do what is good. Jesus laid down His very own life for the sake of the treasure, His redeemed people.*

One further thing I want to point out to you about the field: Jesus bought the field, but He leaves it to His servants, the ministers of the gospel, to recover the treasure. You have to locate the treasure, dig it up, and take it out of the earth. If it has been in the dirt for a very long time, it is rusty, dirty, and sometimes corroded, needing much cleanup.

Jesus sends us out to find the treasure, dig it out, and bring it to Him. Sometimes it is taking a group of redeemed women into strip clubs, on assignment, to bring the hidden treasure out, the lost souls. Many women are held in bondage to the amount of money they can make by working in these places in the world. Men who go there are lost and on their way to hell too.

Paul says in Colossians 1:28–29 that we proclaim Jesus. We proclaim Him, admonishing and teaching everyone with all wisdom, so that we may present everyone perfect in Christ. Paul was not content with leaving any of God's people below their level of potential in God's plan. He worked very hard and went on to say, "To this end I labor, struggling with all His energy, which so powerfully works in me" (NIV).

God's love was extravagant. He did not want to leave one person in the dirt. Everything about God is far greater and grander than we can possibly comprehend. The very nature of God is love. Our human love is not always so nice. It is sometimes short, stingy, and self-centered. But God's love is not like that at all. It is amazing, vast, boundless, and extravagant.

I recommend you study Paul's prayer in Ephesians 3:14–19. God desires to put the fullness of His love in every vessel that He creates by His Holy Spirit. He desires that we come to know Him. He wants us to know all the dimensions of His love—how wide, how long, how high, and how deep it is. He wants us to know a love that surpasses knowledge. God's love is very personal. It is everlasting. It precedes time and is irresistible.

I remember God giving me a scripture when I was a young girl. That scripture was Jeremiah 31:3: "The Lord hath appeared of old unto me, [It is not a new thing—it's from old] saying, Yea, I have loved thee [individually, personally] with an everlasting love: therefore with lovingkindness have I drawn thee." God draws us to Himself.

God's love precedes time. Ephesians 1:4–5: "For He [God] chose us in Him [Christ] before the creation of the world to be holy and blameless in His sight. In love He predestined us to be adopted as His sons through Jesus Christ..." (NIV). Before the creation of the world God loved us. He chose us and arranged the course of our lives so we would encounter Him and encounter His amazing and extravagant love.

God's love is irresistible. Song of Solomon 8:6 says, "Love is as strong as death..." Death is irresistible. When death comes, no one can turn it away.

Solomon says, "Love is as strong as death." In the New Testament, Jesus died and rose from the dead. He proved that love is stronger than death.

What did it mean for Jesus to give His life on our behalf? The price of redemption was the blood of Jesus. The Bible says, "Knowing that you were not redeemed with perishable things like silver or gold from your futile way of life inherited from your forefathers, but with precious blood, as of a lamb unblemished and spotless, the blood of Christ" (1 Peter 1:18–19, NASB).

It was through the blood of Jesus that we could be redeemed from our sin. The life, or soul, of all flesh is in the blood. If a living creature has a soul and has blood, then the life, or soul, of that creature is in its blood. God gave Moses the laws for how to live according to the principles of God. The Bible says, "For the life of the flesh is in the blood, and I have given it to you on the altar to make atonement for your souls; For it is the blood by reason of life [or soul] that makes atonement" (Leviticus 17:11, NASB).

The Hebrew word that is translated for *life* is the Hebrew word for "soul." It was the precious blood of Jesus alone that could propitiate the sins of God's people. God gave His only Son so that we might have life, and life eternal. Isaiah says, "He hath poured out his soul unto death: and he was numbered with the transgressors; and he bare the sin of many, and made intercession for the transgressors" (Isaiah 53:12). We can see the four statements about what Jesus did. Before He died on the cross He prayed, "Father, forgive them for they do not know what they do." He poured out His life for us.

While walking through the desert, you might encounter someone who mistreats you and have to pray that same prayer. I know I have prayed it, and I can assure you it works. People that are lost don't really know they are lost and on their way to hell. Their eyes are blinded by the enemy. Don't give up on anyone. Keep praying for the lost!

God gave His Son Jesus that we might have life. Don't allow the enemy to waste one more day of your life. Satan will try to discourage you from the very basics of your faith to destroy the pursuit of your purpose, your call, and destiny. We must all choose to get back to the basics of God's Word and in our own personal pursuit of Him. Without a basic foundational biblical life, anyone can end up shipwrecked or in a desert. We have all been created with purpose, and from the beginning of time, mankind has always asked the questions, "What am I here for?" and "What is my purpose?" Don't attempt to take shortcuts in your relationship with God. Choose life! Choose God's ways and learn to become a person of influence for God. Whatever God has put in your heart, He has equipped you to do. Find someone who is already doing what God has called you to do and pray for them. Choose to promote them through your words, serving them, or whatever God tells you to do.

What you make happen for others, God will make happen for you. I remember how the Lord placed people in my life who were writing books. God gave me the opportunity to sow into their lives and help promote them through various ways. I distributed and gave away thousands of books before I got married to my husband. After we were married, we continued doing the same. God gave us the opportunity to sow seeds for a harvest. We went from distributing Christian materials to teaching and training pastors in a foreign nation. God uses you for His kingdom when you are available. God expands and enlarges your territory when you commit your ways to Him. The Bible says, "As long as the earth endures, seedtime and harvest, cold and heat, summer and winter, day and night will never cease" (Genesis 8:22, NIV).

God is opening doors for us (God's people) that no man can close. Thank God in advance for doors of opportunity. Every place of opposition and change is a door of opportunity. Your seed is your door out of trouble and negative circumstances. Thank God in every situation and praise Him. Job sowed a prayer of deliverance for his three friends, and then God turned Job's captivity around. Your contribution to someone in trouble always unlocks God's contribution into your life. If you have a dream God has placed in your heart that you have not seen come to fruition, look for someone who is already doing what God has placed in your heart and begin to pray for them. Find a way to sow into their life and promote them. What you make happen for others, God will make happen for you.

"And David built there an altar unto the LORD, and offered burnt offerings and peace offerings. So the LORD was intreated for the land, and the plague was stayed from Israel" (2 Samuel 24:25).

CHAPTER 50

STEP OUT IN FAITH

Let God Shine through You to Others

God wants you to step out and become a person of influence. God wants you and me to flow together in such unity that He is all there is to us. He desires His purpose to be priority in your life and for you to yield to the flow of His Spirit, which will move you to fulfill your destiny in His kingdom. God has a great plan and a mighty call on your life to let Him shine through you to others. Confluence comes as a result of influence. The definition of confluence is coming or flowing together, meeting, or gathering at one point.

Philippians 2:2 says, "Fulfill my joy by being like-minded, having the same love, *being* of one accord, of one mind" (NKJV). Conduct your life as a gospel sermon for observers in your life. You may be the only Bible some people ever read. Choose to develop the heart attitude of unity. Live unselfishly! Love radically! Esteem others as being more important than yourself. Remember the value God places on people. Develop an attitude of gratitude. Become a person of influence for Christ.

Staying plugged into Jesus is the key to growth! This is where the healing begins. No one can take your relationship with Jesus away! Is your focus on things that are eternal or things that are perishable? Keep your focus on Jesus and learn to get excited about the next opportunity to share your faith!

Fix your eyes on Jesus, "the author and finisher of our faith" (Hebrews 12:2). Remember, God is the Master trainer. "He teaches my hands to make war, So that my arms can bend a bow of bronze" (Psalm 18:34, NKJV). He says in His Word, "Above all else, guard your heart, for it is the wellspring of life" (Proverbs 4:23, NIV). When we learn to "watch over" our hearts (our special treasure storehouse), we guard and keep them protected. Remember, you are extremely valuable in God's plan for His kingdom. Your natural treasures are your time, money, feelings, and beliefs. He gives you the opportunity to serve Him for His purpose when you commit your life to Him.

Move from the place of the desert to the spring of healing found in God. Don't allow the past to emotionally cripple and keep you in bondage. God has a great plan for your life! You are His special treasure. God is always up to something exciting in your life and mine! Remember, always stay eternity minded. Keep your eyes fixed on Jesus. Choose to walk in humility. Wisdom is seeing God's perspective.

Because of your relationship with Jesus and the empowerment of His Holy Spirit, you not only can pray and receive God's best for your life, but also you become a living testimony that will do great damage to the kingdom of darkness. The enemy will try to defeat you through false shame. He will also try to arouse as many people as possible to become angry, criticize you, and oppose you; but keep moving forward as a living testimony of God's grace, mercy, love, and healing power.

Choose to walk in humility, especially under attack, and shake it off realizing it is nothing but the devil's tactics to keep you silent. *Unless you tell them, how else will they know* they too can experience freedom? The Bible tells us that where the Spirit of the Lord is, there is freedom. (See 2 Corinthians 3:17.)

Don't fear the disapproval of man so much that you are hindered in stepping out to share your story. Don't bow down to the enemy or the people the enemy uses. Only bow to God! Remember your experience and help others to understand that emotional healing is painful, but not as painful as staying stuck in the past. There is pain of change and also pain in remaining the same. Choose to help others find victory in God's amazing restoration and redemption program. God, the Father, is waiting for His sons and daughters to return to Him. The Bible tells us the story of the prodigal son in Luke 15:11–32. It is a great story of a young man finally coming to his senses and returning to his father. The father was waiting and had the best robe waiting for him, as well as a ring and sandals for his feet. God desires to clothe each of us in His righteousness and places His signet ring on our hand. He places sandals on our feet that are symbolic of our walk with Him through life. Use your story to help others come to their senses and run to Father God!

CLOSING COMMENTS

Be Trustworthy

God exposes hidden secrets to us when we are trustworthy to be trusted with the revelation or assignment from God. (See John 7:18 and Luke 4:11.) Having wrong heart motives is one reason why many disqualify themselves from receiving from God. When we choose to seek glory for ourselves or seek to prove our importance, position, and even ministry, we are walking in pride and not giving glory to God by pointing others to the King of kings and Lord of lords. Learn to discover your purpose in the place of transformation, and don't miss your assignment from God! Turn your eyes toward Jesus and seek Him!

When we truly come to understand the grace of God, which is of far greater value than any earthly position or worldly treasure, we will have a far greater focus on doing things with God and choosing to humble ourselves. (See 1 Corinthians 1:26–30.) God calls those who are weak so He may exhibit His strength. God exhibits His wisdom through those who seek Him with their whole heart. Choose this day whom you will serve! Chase after Him with every fiber of your being. Pray and ask God to allow you to hear Him at the slightest whisper at the door of your heart! He is calling out to you today, no matter if you are having the best time of your life or walking through the desert. We are living in a *kairos* moment of time.[1] God has created us "for such a time as this" (Esther 4:14). God is restoring and releasing His power to the apostolic and miracle-working ministries of His people. Don't allow the enemy to steal one more day from your destiny by keeping you in bondage to the past. God is searching to and fro for men and women with radical faith and total surrender to the Holy Spirit. God is pouring out His Spirit to open your eyes to a new level of faith.

When we abide in His presence, we begin to see His hand in every detail around us. He desires that we seek Him so that we may manifest the hidden treasures of Jesus on earth. You are His precious treasure! It's your time now! Step out in faith. Live large. Love extravagantly. Freely forgive and move forward into your destiny. We are called to be a lighthouse to the world.

—DR. DEBORAH STARCZEWSKI

BIBLIOGRAPHY

Baker, H. A., Visions Beyond the Veil (New Kensington, PA: Whitaker House, 2006).

Baker, Sally A., *Family Violence & The Chemical Connection* (Deerfield Beach, FL: Health Communications, 1991).

Concord First Assembly (CFA), Mission Statement, Concord, North Carolina.

Copeland, Germaine, *Prayers That Avail Much*, 25th Anniversary Edition (Rosswell, GA: Word Ministries, 1977).

Internet website: yada-yahweh.org, Content copyright 2011, Yada Yahweh Ministries, Mansfield, Texas.

Pohlmann, Lisa, Skeek Frazee, and Merril Cousin, *Questions to ask yourself: "Am I being abused?" Information Guide for Abused Women in Maine* (n.p.: Main Division, American Association of University Women, 1988). Listed in Family Violence & The Chemical Connection (Basic questions in abuse literature).

Post-Traumatic Stress Disorder: *The American Journal of Psychiatry*/Articles – Also from personal experience after trauma. *Trivita's Wellness Report*, by Brazos Minshew, Trivita's Chief Science Officer: *Stressed Out? It Could Make You Gain Weight*, WWR 213.

Random House College Dictionary Revised Edition (New York: Random House, 1980).

Renner, Rick, *Sparkling Gems from the Greek* (n.p.: Teach All Nations, Rick Renner Ministries). Recommended daily devotional.

Scholar's Library Gold: LOGOS Software System

Strong, James, *The New Strong's Guide to Bible Words: English Index to Hebrew and Greek Words* (Nashville, TN: Thomas Nelson Publishers, 2008).

Strong, James, *The New Strong's Exhaustive Concordance of the Bible* (Nashville, TN: Thomas Nelson Publishers, 1990).

Vine, W.E. *Vines Complete Expository Dictionary of Old and New Testament Words* (Nashville, TN: Thomas Nelson Publishers, 1996).

Endnotes

Chapter 6
EMOTIONAL AND VERBAL ABUSE

1. Sally A. Baker, *Family Violence & The Chemical Connection* (Deerfield Beach, FL: Health Communications, 1991).

2. *Ibid.*

3. *Ibid.*

4. *Ibid.*

5. *Ibid.*

Chapter 7
SEXUAL SIN AND SEDUCTIONS EXPOSED

1. *Random House College Dictionary Revised Edition* (New York: Random House, 1980), 19, s.v. "adultery."

2. W. E. Vine, *Vines Complete Expository Dictionary of Old and New Testament Words* (Nashville, TN: Thomas Nelson Publishers, 1996), 252, s.v. "porneia."

3. *Ibid.*, 291, s.v. "porne."

4. *Ibid.*, 252, s.v. "pornos."

5. *Random House College Dictionary Revised Edition*, 1033, s.v. "pornography."

6. *Ibid.*, 519, s.v. "fornication."

7. *Ibid.*, 1429, s.v. "unclean."

Chapter 8
SEASONS IN LIFE

1   *Random House College Dictionary Revised Edition*, 636, s.v. "honor."

2   *Ibid.*, 380, s.v. "dishonor."

Chapter 13
KNOWING GOD AS FATHER

1.   James Strong, *The New Strong's Exhaustive Concordance of the Bible*, (Nashville, TN: Thomas Nelson Publishers, 1990), Strong's #7355. See also "racham," http://www.bibletools.org/index.cfm/fuseaction/Lexicon.show/ID/H7355/racham.htm#ixzz1TMhYm8Fc.

Chapter 18
SECRETS TO SUCCESS

1.   H. A. Baker, *Visions Beyond the Veil* (New Kensington, PA: Whitaker House, 2006).

Chapter 22
SEEING GOD'S PROVISION

1.   Germaine Copeland, *Prayers That Avail Much*, 25th Anniversary Edition (Rosswell, GA: Word Ministries, 1977), 530.

Chapter 28
WE ARE A TEAM WITH GOD

1.   *Random House College Dictionary Revised Edition*, (New York: Random House, 1980), 1124, s.v. "respire."

2.   *Ibid.*, s.v. "respiration."

Chapter 29
PRAYER AND WORSHIP

1.   *The Maxwell Leadership Bible* (Nashville, TN: Thomas Nelson, 2002), 318.

CHAPTER 30
FEELING FORSAKEN

1.   *The New Strong's Exhaustive Concordance of the Bible*, Strong's # 3056.

2.   *Ibid.*, Strong's #5800.

Chapter 39
MINISTRY OF HEALING

1. James Strong, *The New Strong's Guide to Bible Words: English Index to Hebrew and Greek Words*, (Nashville, TN: Thomas Nelson Publishers, 2008), s.v. "sophroneo."

CLOSING COMMENTS

1. *Vines Complete Expository Dictionary of Old and New Testament Words*, 726, s.v. "kairos."

ABOUT THE AUTHOR

Dr. Deborah Starczewski is enthusiastic, down to earth, compassionate, and humorous. She impacts the lives of everyone she encounters. Deborah inspires others with wisdom, motivation, and hope in God with a strong gifting in the prophetic.

Having personally experienced heartache, pain, and rejection, Deborah understands the challenges that often accompany everyday life. She focuses on knowing God and exemplifying Him to others as she imparts truth through the Word, believing that everyone has been created by God for a divine purpose. Her message is powerful and her testimonies of God's supernatural intervention are miraculous! She will inspire you to seek God for yourself as she shares her wisdom and insight into the heart of God. Her life experiences of redemption and restoration give hope to all. Deborah's compassion is founded in the heart of Jesus!

Deborah's real life experiences, though extremely painful, have given her the ability to identify with the hurting, brokenhearted, and those who don't understand what on earth is going on in their lives. Out of her own personal encounters with Jesus, she formed two conclusions that will never change: first, that Jesus Christ is alive; second, that the Bible is a true, relevant, up-to-date book. What matters most to Deborah is seeing lives changed, hearts healed, and destinies fulfilled for those who dare to dream and step out into God's plan for their life. Deborah tells you what the Word says and encourages you to know God for yourself. Her message is real and life transforming. Be prepared to change!

Deborah founded Star Ministries, Inc., based on John 2:5: "Whatever He says to you, do it" on April 21, 1998; and a nonprofit organization,

Star National Outreach Worldwide, Inc., in 2008 based on Psalm 51:7 and taking the gospel to the nations. She finished extensive training and earned her doctorate at Life Christian University. She has a heart for God and people. She is a teacher at her church, a local Christian University, and is also a conference speaker. Deborah and her husband have also ministered and traveled abroad. She also has a heart for the nations! She loves imparting truth from God's Word and praying for the sick and afflicted. She loves God, loves people, and passes it on!

Deborah and Dan have been married for fifteen years with two children in their blended family. She has one son, one stepdaughter, and four grandchildren. Deborah believes we have all been created to be ministers, cleverly disguised in whatever sphere of influence we find ourselves.

To contact the author write:

Dr. Deborah Starczewski

Star National Outreach Worldwide, Inc.

PO Box 70

Cornelius, NC 28031

Email: deborah@starministriesinc.com

www.starministriesinc.com